T0065651

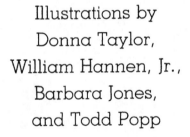

Illustrations by
Donna Taylor,
William Hannen, Jr.,
Barbara Jones,
and Todd Popp

A FIRESIDE BOOK
PUBLISHED BY SIMON & SCHUSTER
New York London Toronto Sydney Tokyo Singapore

The
Perfectly
Safe
Home

JEANNE E. MILLER

Fireside

Simon & Schuster Building
Rockefeller Center
1230 Avenue of the Americas
New York, New York 10020

Designed by Mary Sarah Quinn
Manufactured in the United States of America

1   3   5   7   9   10   8   6   4   2   Pbk.

Library of Congress Cataloging-in-Publication Data
Miller, Jeanne E.
The perfectly safe home / Jeanne E. Miller ; illustrations by
Donna Taylor . . . [et al.].
p.   cm.
Includes bibliographical references and index.
1. Home accidents—Prevention.   2. Children's accidents—
Prevention.   I. Title.
TX150.M55   1991
649'.1'0289—dc20   91-4711   CIP
ISBN 0-671-70580-6 Pbk.

For Mom, who safely raised seven children and taught me, her eldest, the importance of the care and nurturing of children
and
For Dad, who taught me I could do anything if I put my mind to it and that "anything worth doing is worth doing well"
and
For Bill, my husband, who believes in me and my causes and is always there to help me out when I get stuck.

Their years of combined effort, support, and love are what really made this book possible.

CONTENTS

Introduction

·AS NEW PARENTS YOUR CHILD IS THE MOST
precious thing in the world to you, and the most vulnerable
of human beings. From infancy through his preschool years
you must be ever vigilant in protecting your child from potential hurts and upsets.

This book is dedicated to helping you keep your child out
of harm's way. The task may seem overwhelming at times
when you realize that tiny fingers, for instance, are fair game
for doors that pinch, stoves that burn, and glass that can cut
or scratch tender skin. In fact, many of the objects and
furnishings you take for granted around your house—in the
kitchen, the bathroom, the family room, and even your own
backyard—can be hidden perils for your child.

In infancy, your child is completely helpless. As she
grows and develops, she acquires a powerful natural drive
to touch, to taste, to try, and to discover new things about
the world around her. As her world expands, the risks mul-
tiply. The more you know about the potential hazards in
what you may have formerly thought of as your "safe" house,
the better prepared you will be to protect your child.

You may already be aware of some of the precautions
noted in this book; others you may never have anticipated.

I hope that these tips and reminders will help you protect your child from a fearful experience, unnecessary tears, a painful hurt, or a life-threatening danger.

By putting this advice into practice, you will reap added benefits: You will become less apprehensive about bringing up your baby, you will feel more relaxed and self-assured about the process, and you will be better able to enjoy your child . . . knowing he or she is perfectly safe.

Jeanne E. Miller

I

Childproofing
Your Home

1

The Perfectly Safe Family

If you could see through your child's eyes, you would see a wonderful and exciting world full of interest and challenge

CHILDHOOD IS FULL of adventure. If you could see through your child's eyes, you would see a wonderful and exciting world full of interest and challenge. If you could feel what your child feels, you would feel curious, impatient, and impulsive.

While these important qualities of curiosity, impatience, and impulsiveness are the very things that motivate your child to learn and develop, they are also the qualities that can steer your child toward trouble. Your responsibility as a parent is to create a safe environment for your child, to teach your child about safety, and to set a good example by practicing safety yourself. It's unrealistic to expect that you can prevent every bump, bruise, and scrape, but you can significantly lower the risk of serious injury to your child.

Practicing safety is not difficult or costly. What it requires is a lot of common sense, the knowledge of what to watch for and what to avoid, some planning and attention to detail, and constant vigilance. Here are the basic steps to follow in your safety program:

- Know when accidents are likeliest to happen and what the biggest dangers are to your child through each stage of his development.
- Be vigilant and never underestimate your child's ability to get into trouble. Always be prepared for the unexpected.
- Find the dangers in and around your home and if you can't eliminate them, at least know how to avoid them. Select only products and equipment with the latest safety advances, use them properly and safely, and never consider them a substitute for adult supervision.
- Think safety. Make safety a habit in your family. Teach your child to think and practice safety.

When Accidents Happen Most

Statistics tell us that most children's accidents happen early in the morning before parents are up and late in the day when parents are rushed or busy. In fact, Saturday is the worst accident day, especially between 3 and 6 P.M. These are the times when supervision is more likely to be lax or nonexistent. In addition to lack of supervision, these factors can contribute to accidents:

Hunger and Fatigue. When children are hungry or tired they are more prone to have an accident—an hour before mealtime, late in the afternoon, and just before bedtime. When a parent or babysitter is tired, they are also more likely to be off guard.

Sudden Change of Environment. Moving to a new house, vacationing, and visiting can throw off the daily routine for both parents and children. There are many new distractions and hazards.

A Change in Routine. A new babysitter or an ill parent can cause a change in routine. Death, divorce, quarreling, and other traumatic changes or conflicts will affect the daily routine or the emotional climate of the home.

Lack of Anticipation. A parent or guardian who does not expect the unexpected from a child can be caught off guard. Many doctors and emergency personnel have heard frustrated comments like these: "I didn't know he could roll over," or "I had no idea she could crawl up stairs, she never did that before." When it comes to children, there is a first time for everything—that's why vigilance is a top priority.

Lack of Educating the Child. A small child who is warned that he'll be spanked if he plays around the stove will reach into a hot oven while looking over his shoulder to see if he's being watched—unaware of the real danger of being seriously burned. Once children are old enough to understand, they must be given specific explanations for why they should or shouldn't do things. At 18 months old, most children can quickly learn what "hot" is—at 2 years old they can begin to appreciate the hazards of traffic. They must be taught to understand the real danger, and not simply to fear punishment.

Protecting Your Child Through Each Stage of Development

Though this book covers most of the hazards your child is likely to encounter from birth through preschool, there are certain dangers and safety recommendations that should be emphasized for children when they are at particular stages of development. When a specific age group is referred to here, please keep in mind as well that every baby has her own personal developmental pace—every child is unique. This makes it very important that you never underestimate your child's ability to get into trouble. You must be vigilant, alert, and always expect the unexpected.

BIRTH TO 4 MONTHS

Between birth and 4 months of age your infant will mostly be interested in eating and sleeping. For amusement he will enjoy touching, holding, batting, turning, shaking, kicking, mouthing, and tasting objects. Most of his time will be spent in his crib and his only other major activities will involve diaper changing, bathing, and eating. At about 3 or 4 months old he will surprise you when he learns how to roll over without assistance and he will delight you when he discovers his feet and learns how his rattle works.

The biggest dangers to children at this age are falls from furniture, water accidents while bathing, auto accidents, choking on food or small objects, and suffocation usually caused by bed clothes or other items left in the crib or playpen. Many of the important safety rules for your infant at this age are in the Nursery, Bathroom, and Furniture and Equipment chapters (Chapters 3, 4, and 6). In these chapters I cover safe bathing for infants, safe diaper changing, and how to safely select and use infant furniture and equipment.

5 TO 7 MONTHS

Your baby is now on the move. At 5 months she is rolling from back to side to stomach and back again. Her manual dexterity is increasing and she can grab and grasp things with fair ability. Anything in her hand goes into her mouth— taste testing is a top priority. At 6 to 7 months she is sitting up and she's becoming a master at the art of crumbling food and banging anything that is remotely bangable. Rolling, scooting, rocking, and bouncing are high on the list of favorite activities. She's beginning to become curious about the world around her and she'll crawl for anything that suits her fancy.

The biggest dangers to children at this age are stairs, electrical cords and outlets, falls from furniture or down stairs, choking on small objects found within reach, auto accidents, poisoning by household products and plants, and water accidents both indoors and out. By the time your child has reached this age, your house and yard should be "childproofed" and safety procedures should be in place and in practice.

8 MONTHS TO 1 YEAR

Your child's growth will be dramatic during this period of his life and keeping up with him will be quite a challenge. At about 9 months old he'll be pulling himself up to a standing position and will be fairly steady at it as long as he has something to hold on to. By about 10 months he'll be able to "walk" with assistance. He'll discover a fascination for things that disappear and reappear again and one of his favorite games will be to look for things that are out of sight. Another favorite interest will be in container/contained relationships—he'll discover the joy of emptying cupboards, drawers, and anything else that holds objects.

Your child's natural curiosity will prompt him to reach and grab, and now that he's able to pull himself to a standing position, his world has expanded to include almost every potential danger listed in this book. But of special concern are poisonous and otherwise dangerous household products, utensils, and medicines stored in cupboards, cabinets, and closets. Burns caused by grabbing for hot drinks or plates, stoves, heaters, and other hot appliances are a real concern. Stair and furniture climbing will become a favorite sport that must be closely supervised to avoid falls. And because he's not very steady on his feet yet, you must look out for nasty tumbles that could cause head injuries. Car rides will hold more interest for him and he may become less inclined to stay in his car seat—but be firm and stick to the automobile safety rules in the chapter on travel safety (Chapter 14).

1-YEAR-OLDS

At about 1 year of age your child will be able to pull herself to her feet and walk with assistance. Her creeping, crawling, and climbing will shift to high gear and her curiosity will reach new heights. At about 1½ she'll be walking alone and will be able to stoop to pick up things on the ground. She'll be capable of tossing objects at an intended target and drinking from a cup without much spilling. She will discover cause and effect, and it will be one of her favorite pastimes to play with things that move or can be made to move—including sand and water. She will begin to imitate adults, especially in caretaking and housekeeping tasks.

When your child is at this age you must be especially careful to supervise her both indoors and out when around any water sources, because her fascination with water will be very strong now. Doors leading to outdoors, the basement, the garage, and other "off-limits" areas must be secured safely because she'll learn how to open doors during this period. Since she'll start imitating adults it is very important that you set good examples of safe behavior to begin the training your child needs in safety techniques.

YOUNG TODDLERS (2 TO 3 YEARS OLD)

From age 2 to 3 your child will be quickly developing and improving his physical and mental skills. He will learn to run better and faster, jump, kick, swing, skip, and dance. He'll begin to repeat your words and put sentences together, he'll learn the difference between "mine" and "yours," and he'll become determined to explore the great big world outside.

Your toddler's mobility and newfound outdoor world bring with them a new age of potential accidents. Now is the time you must begin to talk with your child about safety. Explain to him what you are doing to protect him and why it is necessary. Involve him in the safety effort and teach him to practice sound safety habits.

Eliminating the Dangers to Your Child

This book will take you, step by step, on a "safety tour" of your home. We'll examine each room from a safety standpoint, and I'll suggest easy-to-follow steps toward childproofing your home.

While you're on your tour and during your childproofing process, please keep in mind three important rules for your child's safety:

1. *The "What-If" Rule.* You may have put a safety latch on the door to the garage, but what if your child finds her way in there? Are the dangerous things placed

out of her reach or locked up? You have installed a lock on the bathroom door, but what if someone forgets to lock it? Have you made sure your water temperature is set lower so it can't burn, does the toilet have a lid-locking device, are all the medicines and cleaning supplies up high out of reach and locked up? The "what-if" rule gives you an extra margin of safety for your child.

2. *The "No-Substitutes" Rule.* There are absolutely no substitutes for a parent's loving care and kind attention. Furniture and baby equipment can't substitute. Manufactured safety devices can't substitute. Children's safety equipment, furniture, and safety devices are part of the "what-if" rule and make the responsibility of caring for your child easier and more manageable, but they're not intended to replace careful supervision and vigilance.

3. *The Golden Rule of Child Safety.* "If it's there, your child will find it. If it can be done, your child will do it." Never underestimate your child's ability to innocently put himself in harm's way. Children have the capacity to pay infinite attention to detail. So use your imagination, look at the world through the eyes of your child, and never stop looking for potential hazards that could threaten your child's safety.

Thinking Safety

In the course of this book not only will you examine each room of your home with an eye toward childproofing, but you will also discover useful hints, tips, and procedures that promote safety. Some may surprise you, while others will seem obvious—but they are all presented with one thought in mind: Safety must become automatic, part of your daily routine. When you reach this point, you'll have achieved what some people refer to as "unconscious competence" or the seemingly natural ability to do just the right thing at the right time. When you have reached this level of unconscious competence and safety has become automatic, you will be able to deal with your child in a more relaxed manner and you will notice that your child feels more relaxed, too. You will have arrived at a careful balance so that your child does not feel overprotected and yet is not unnecessarily exposed to danger. And when proper attention is paid to "thinking safety" and practicing safety, your child will learn this, too. She will come to anticipate hazards, and thinking about safety will become a part of her developing habits. And in the last analysis, that's what this book is all about.

Childproofing Your Home

The dangers to your baby are legion given his natural abundance of curiosity

THE BEST RULE for child-proofing your home is to plan it carefully and do it in advance. Unfortunately, in many cases, the importance of childproofing is apparent only after a child's accident or near-accident.

When he learns how to open the basement door and just about tumbles down the steps, door security becomes pretty high on your list of priorities. His little finger going for an electrical outlet points out the need for outlet protection . . . and so on. During your child's younger years you'll learn that life can be a thrill a minute, and the dangers to your baby are legion given his natural abundance of curiosity at this point in time.

While there is no substitute for your close attention, there are things that you can do to make your house a safer place for your child to grow and play in. If you do this carefully and well in advance, you can minimize some of those split-second dangers to your safety and make this period less harrowing and more pleasant for the entire family.

This chapter deals with the more common aspects found in any room: doors, windows, electrical outlets, stairs, and so on. Generally speaking, there are a number of inexpensive items that can be purchased for childproofing purposes. These, combined with many helpful hints and safety practices, will go a long way toward making your home a safer place for your child.

Electrical Safety

When people think of childproofing their homes, electrical safety comes quickly to mind. And well it should, because a 110-volt shock to a small child can be more than frightening—it's downright dangerous.

All electrical outlets within your small child's reach *must* be covered. This is very important. There are many difference devices made for this purpose. When you are selecting outlet covers, make sure the covers are of good quality so they will endure your use and your child's persistent efforts to open them.

Outlet covers are available in four basic styles and are

easy to install by removing the screw holding the wall plate, and replacing or covering the wall plate with the outlet cover.

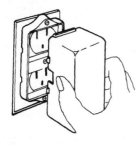

TO REMOVE A SNAP-ON OUTLET COVER requires a strong squeeze to disengage the locking tabs at the sides. When the cover is replaced the locking tabs snap back into place. This style is the most difficult for children to learn to open because it relies more on strength than ingenuity. The best snap-on covers have boxes that are deep enough to accommodate grounded (the large three-pronged type) appliance plugs.

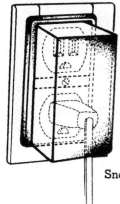

Snap-on outlet cover

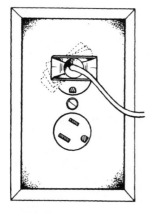

Twist-style outlet cover

THE TWIST-STYLE OUTLET COVER automatically twists closed when a plug is removed. To use the outlet you insert the plug prongs into the slots in the safety plate, turn the plug clockwise, and then push it into the outlet. When the plug is removed, the plate automatically twists to close off the outlet, giving protection even if an appliance is unplugged by your child.

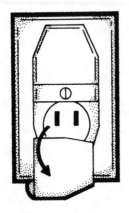

Spring-loaded outlet cover

SPRING-LOADED OUT-LET COVERS require some strength and finger dexterity to open and they automatically snap closed when the plug is pulled out. Some models have a built-in, tamperproof, flat nightlight in one of the sockets. These are recommended for locations where a nightlight is required but the outlet is within your child's reach, making a regular nightlight a safety concern.

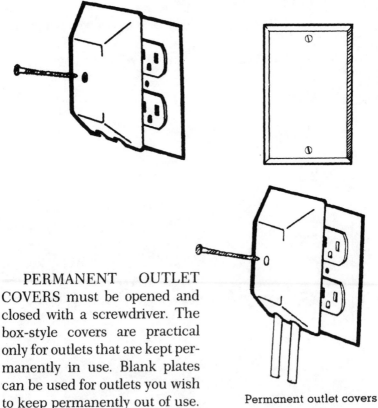

PERMANENT OUTLET COVERS must be opened and closed with a screwdriver. The box-style covers are practical only for outlets that are kept permanently in use. Blank plates can be used for outlets you wish to keep permanently out of use.

Permanent outlet covers

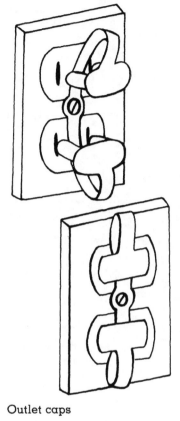

Outlet caps

OUTLET CAPS are plastic two-pronged disks that fit into an existing outlet. They are a quick, easy, and inexpensive way of offering short-term protection for your child in a hotel room or while visiting friends and relatives. When purchasing these caps, test them to make sure they are extremely tight-fitting and are made of UL-approved plastic. Outlet caps are not recommended for long-term, continued use because they may become too loose-fitting and children learn quickly how to pull them out. And in most cases, when these caps are removed from the outlet they are easily misplaced, leaving the outlet exposed, and they are small enough to present a choking hazard. To avoid these two problems, it's best to select the type that attaches to the outlet plate screw with a tether strap, such as the one in the illustration.

ELECTRICAL CORDS

Keeping electrical cords out of reach has been a challenge to parents for nearly 100 years. The most common injuries caused by electrical cords are burns to the mouth and face when a child chews on the cord. And while there is no such thing as completely childproofing an electrical cord, there are some things you can do to reduce the potential dangers to your child:

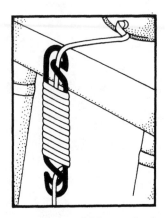

Cord shorteners

- Cords running along the floor or wall should be tacked down with insulated staples or taped down with strong tape.
- USE PLASTIC CORD SHORTENERS or electrical tape to wind up the excess electrical cord and tuck it out of reach.
- Avoid the use of extension cords. If an extension cord is necessary, wrap electrical tape around the connection so the appliance plug cannot be pulled out of the extension cord. Never leave an extension cord plugged in at one end and exposed on the other end, and never plug a three-pronged plug into a two-hole extension cord.
- See that electrical cords and extension cords are never located in your child's normal traveling path.
- Lamp cords and other small appliance cords that dangle from tables should be secured so your child cannot tug the cord and pull down the appliance. Try moving the table tight against the wall with the cord wedged between the wall and table or secure the dangling cord with a cord guard designed for this purpose. If all else fails, move the lamp or appliance to another location where the cord will not be within reach.
- Remember that telephones work on electricity. When you're securing your other electrical cords, take care of the phone cords, too.

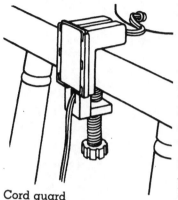

Cord guard

B. ELECTRICITY AND WATER

Electricity, by its nature, always seeks the earth or "ground" by the most efficient means. Every electrical socket contains a positive socket and a "ground" socket, so that the flow of current through any appliance is completed to the "ground" socket.

Water, by its nature, is a good and very efficient conductor of electricity, and if the normal flow of current through an appliance is interrupted, water can conduct the flow of electricity to the "ground" by alternate paths. For example, the extreme danger of standing in a wet bathtub with a hair dryer is that the current will not flow to the normal "ground" socket at the outlet, but will instead pass through your body, through the water, and proceed to the "ground" by using the water pipes.

A ground-fault circuit interrupter is a device that helps prevent electrical shock by detecting flows of current through such unintended paths. When the GFCI, as it is called, detects such an electrical fault, it quickly shuts off the flow of electrical current before serious injury can occur.

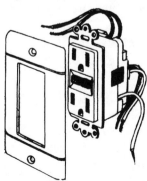

Ground fault circuit interrupter (GFCI)

MORE TIPS ON ELECTRICAL SAFETY

- Never leave light-bulb sockets empty when lamps are plugged in and check to make sure the bulbs are securely tightened.
- Don't leave hair dryers or other similar appliances plugged in when not being used. Many people do not realize this, but even with the switch off, a plugged-in appliance that falls into water can electrify the water. So never use any electrical appliances near a tub, sink, or pool.
- Keep electrical fans and heaters up and out of your child's reach.
- If your electrical breaker or fuse box is within your child's reach, lock it up. Most electrical boxes are equipped with a place for a padlock.
- Never allow your child to play with electrical appliances. Don't purchase electrically operated toys for your child until she is old enough (see Chapter 7 on toys), and always supervise your child when she is playing with electrical toys.

Door and Entryway Safety

Every door in your home will offer an interesting challenge to your young child—to open it, go through to the other side, and close it behind him. He won't mind a bit that what's on the other side may be dangerous, and if he can't get back he just has to call for Mommy. Early on, he won't understand the workings of the door, so it's not unlikely that he'll put a few fingers in the jamb while pushing the door shut with the other hand.

To control this process of experimentation, door safety has some basic elements: Secure the doors that should be secured, make unsecured doors safe by allowing easy access from either side, and take precautions against pinching.

Check all the interior doors in your home to make sure that none can be locked from the inside without access from the outside. If some have locks, find the keys. Doors with push-button locks should have a small hole on the outside knob. A piece of coat hanger or a large hairpin inserted in the hole will unlock the door. Keep the key or unlocking device handy by hanging it high out of your child's reach on a nail just outside the door. Now, if your child should lock himself in, you will have quick access to the room.

If you discover that you have a door that is lockable but it does not have a key or is not equipped with a lock-release hole, it is best that you have the lock replaced. In the meantime, a towel thrown over the top of the door will keep the door from closing tightly. Just make sure the towel is high enough that your child can't pull it off.

Exterior doors and doors to an attached garage should be kept closed and locked or latched at all times. Before your child learns to unlock these exterior doors, install extra latches up high out of her reach. In fact, any door that leads to a stairway or other area that is unsafe for your child should be considered for extra latches—closets and storage rooms, attic, bathroom, basement, porch. Your hardware store should have a large selection of locking and latching hardware for you to choose from, but make sure these devices are not difficult to install or inconvenient to use. Here are some solutions for door security that have been specifically designed for child safety and for easy installation and use:

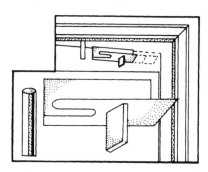

Safety door latch

Safety door latches are designed to fit over the top of an interior door of standard thickness. The latching and unlatching mechanism can be accessed from both sides of the door. This latch has advantages over a standard hardware slide latch because it requires only one latch rather than one on each side of the door, and because it can be accessed by another adult without the necessity of having to unlock it for them from your side.

This device is good for doors leading to the garage or basement, for example, where adults and older children may be going in and out a lot. If one adult comes up the basement stairs he can unlatch the door from the basement side and then relatch it from the other side. If another adult is still in the basement, he can then unlatch it himself from the basement side—in other words, he's not locked in the basement. The only alternatives to this device are:

1. A deadbolt that works from both sides—but the child would eventually learn to use it once he can reach it
2. A key lock—but all adults would have to carry a key with them
3. Hook and eye on both sides—someone could be locked in or out if on the other side of the door
4. A safety gate—but the door would have to remain open

A doorknob cover fits over an existing doorknob. Unless it is gripped tightly by an adult or older child, the cover turns but the doorknob does not. This makes it impossible for your toddler to open the door until he is old enough to have the strength to squeeze the cover sufficiently.

The slide lock works for cabinet, closet, or utility-room doors (including sliding or accordion-type doors) that have side-by-side pull handles or knobs. It slides over or inside both handles or knobs and has a catch that you tighten against the outermost knob or handle. To remove the slide catch requires more strength than your small child can muster.

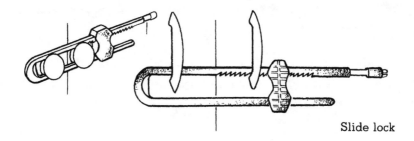

Slide lock

GLASS DOORS

Sliding glass doors—windows that reach close to the floor—and glass storm doors should be considered carefully. Make sure the glass is safety glass—it should say so in one of the corners of the glass if it is. Should you find that your child often forgets there is glass there and bumps his head trying to walk or crawl "through" it, try applying decals on the glass at his eye level. This will help remind him it's a "dead end."

In warmer weather when the sliding glass door is open, make sure the screen is closed and locked. If the screen is not equipped with a lock, try using a pole or board in the track of the screen door to keep it from being opened. Depending on how your door is designed, this may require going outside by another exit to "lock" and "unlock" the screen but it may be better than the alternative of keeping the glass door closed and locked.

There are a few handy sliding door safety devices available to help with the problems associated with sliding doors. One sliding door lock/alarm is equipped with a security bar that prevents both entry and exit. It can be used to lock the door completely closed or allows you to leave the door slightly open for ventilation. This device also has an optional alarm that will warn you if an intruder tries to push open the door from the ouside or your child attempts to remove the bar lock from the track.

Another type of locking bar, sometimes referred to as a "charley bar," works for both sliding doors and windows. When the bar is in its locked or "down" position it wedges a sliding door or window shut. When the bar is in its "open" or raised position, the sliding door or window can be moved. These devices are available at many hardware stores or home centers and are very easy to install.

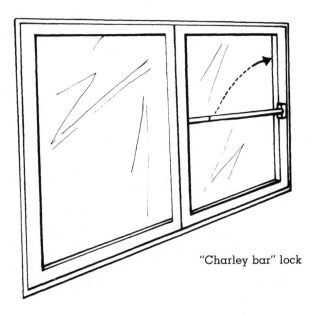

"Charley bar" lock

Automatic sliding-door closers are the best solution to the problem of family members who forget to close doors, leaving an open invitation to a small child to follow them outside. These door closers are very easy to install, require no batteries or electricity, and are equipped with a "hold-open" switch and adjustable speed control to help prevent the door from slamming shut. Some models also have locks to prevent the door from being opened by anyone too short to reach the top door track.

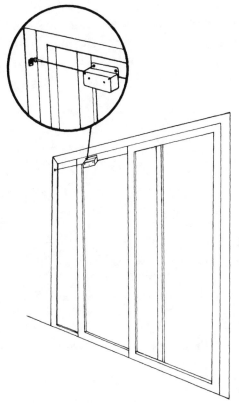

Automatic sliding-door closer

SWINGING DOORS

Swinging or cafe-style doors can be a menace to your crawling or toddling child. Until your child is past the toddler stage, it is best to fasten these doors in an open position by installing a hook-and-eye device, or remove the doors completely. If the doors lead to an off-limits area such as the kitchen or laundry room, make sure to install a security gate in their place.

SOLUTIONS TO PINCHING AND SLAMMING SITUATIONS

To keep your child safe from being pinched by doors, try these solutions:

Conventional and Swinging Doors. Prevent pinching from conventional and swinging doors by hanging a washcloth over the top hinges or by using a door stopper such as the one shown in the illustration to stop the door from closing completely.

Sliding Doors. To avoid finger pinching in interior sliding doors, install a rubber door bumper at the top or bottom of the doorjamb large enough to keep fingers safe, or nail a small block of wood in the corner on the lower track that will interfere with the door completely closing.

Accordion Doors. This type of door is not only a pinching menace, but it is difficult for young children to operate. They can easily get themselves on the wrong side of the door and not understand how to open it. To solve both problems, use the door stoppers mentioned for conventional doors, locating one between each panel. This way the accordion door will not close tightly and also your child will have a hint whether to push or pull in order to get the door opened.

If you have doors that can be slammed by sudden drafts, use wedges to keep them propped open so they won't slam on your baby, shutting her out or startling her. Make sure the wedges are made of a safe, nontoxic rubber, just in case your child finds one on an excursion around the floor.

Of course, if any of these doors leads to an area that is off-limits to your child, the door should not be propped open but kept locked or latched at all times.

SECURITY GATES

In open doorways leading to stairs or rooms that are dangerous for your child to be crawling or playing in, install security gates, which come in a vast array of styles and sizes. There are even some available to fit extra-wide archways and openings. When using a security gate, follow these important safety guidelines:

- Select a safe security gate and try to avoid used gates. Refer to Chapter 6 for information about selecting a proper gate.
- If you use a pressure gate, make sure to install it with the pressure bar on the side away from your child. He may try to use the pressure bar for climbing.
- Never install a pressure gate at the top of steps or a flight of stairs. There is always the possibility the gate could become loose and cause a fall if your child leans against it.
- Never close a gate without latching it securely. Your child will probably develop the habit of leaning against the security gate and if it isn't latched, she could take a spill.
- Follow the manufacturer's instructions very carefully when installing and using security gates. Most recommend that you should discontinue use of a security gate when your child reaches about 2 years old or when he is old enough to climb or pivot over it. This will depend on the height and strength of the gate and your child's rate of development.

Window Safety

The windows of your home should be checked very carefully. It's obvious that your child should not have access to the outside through a window, but there are a few other considerations to keep in mind also. Check every window in your home using this eight-point checklist:

1. Make sure there is no furniture placed under windows that your child could use for climbing up to the window.
2. Check all screens to see that they are strongly in place and free of holes or torn spots. See that they are safely locked and that they cannot be pushed up or out by your child.

3. Every window should have a latch that is high out of your child's reach. Windows above ground level should be equipped with window guards or safety latches—never depend on screens to withstand your child's weight.

4. Window blind and drapery cords should be wound up and placed high out of your child's reach. Entanglement in cords has caused harm to many small children.

5. Check venetian blind slats very carefully. Some styles have thin, sharp edges that could cut a baby's tender skin. Remove blinds of this kind until your child is much older or remember to keep the blinds rolled up high beyond your child's reach.

6. When you remove storm windows, be sure to store them away in a safe place where your child cannot reach them.

7. If you have double-hung windows that can open from the top, make a practice of always opening them from the top.

8. To prevent your child from opening crank-out windows, remove the crank handles. This makes it very difficult for a young child to open the windows.

WINDOW LATCHES AND WINDOW GUARDS

Safety latches and window guards come in dozens of varieties and designs, but they basically serve one of two purposes. Safety latches prevent a window from being opened or from being opened past a certain point; most hardware stores have a variety of styles for all types of windows. Window guards are made for windows of all styles and are installed inside the frame to prevent entry or exit while still allowing the window to be opened all the way. The rails on window guards and the distance a window is set open with a safety latch should never exceed 4 inches. That is the safe distance to insure your child cannot climb through or get himself trapped in the opening.

It is important to note here that window grates, guards, or latches that cannot be opened or removed quickly should not be used on windows that may be needed as an escape in case of fire.

If you have sliding windows, you can also use many of the same devices discussed earlier in this chapter for use on sliding doors.

Sliding window

Stationary Panel

Double-hung window

Window guards

Casement window

A 12-Point Furniture Checklist

If you're like most people, you are probably so used to your home furnishings that you hardly notice them anymore. You know they're there, you have the locations memorized, and though there may be a few flaws you work around them in your normal daily routine.

But to your crawling baby or toddler who has just discovered the thrill of motion, this is all new. Even a loose tack in the upholstery is something to be examined, and new heights can be achieved by climbing up the chairs to get to the dining-room table.

While every home's furnishings vary widely and must be considered individually, you can start by using this 12-point checklist for safety:

1. Check the drawers in all your furniture and built-in cabinets. Make sure they have safety catches to prevent the drawers from being pulled all the way out.

2. Make sure that every drawer, cabinet, cupboard, or shelf that is accessible to your child contains nothing of a dangerous nature, or secure it with a latching or locking device. A drawer in the family room may contain pencils or matches, one in your bedroom may hold reading glasses or medicine. The hutch in the dining room may be full of breakable china or glass. Refer to Chapter 5 on kitchens for information about securing drawers, cupboards, and cabinets.

3. If you have bookshelves, clear the shelves that are reachable by your child or squeeze the books in very tightly so your child cannot pull them down on herself. If the shelves reach to the floor and could be used as a ladder, move another piece of furniture in front of the shelves to discourage your child from trying this.

4. Clear all tables and lower shelves of items such as ashtrays, matches or lighters, pipe tobacco or ciga-

rettes, dried or live flower arrangements, and glass dishes and figurines.

5. If you have glass table tops, remove heavy objects that your child could possibly use to smash the glass. And be prepared for the possibility that your child will crawl under the table and then try to sit or stand up, not realizing the glass is there. The best solution for this, if it keeps happening, is to cover the glass with a nontoxic adhesive fabric of some kind.

6. Sharp edges and corners on furniture can cause serious bumps and cuts when a child falls against them. If a piece of furniture is dangerously sharp, it's best to remove it until your child is past the toddler stage. Other pieces can be made safer by using a cushioning foam or fabric and taping it with wide tape to the corners and edges. Or there are edge and corner cushions you can purchase that are made specifically for this purpose.

7. Also check the undersides of all tables for sharp edges and dangerous protrusions such as nails, screws, or bolts and eliminate or cover any you find. If there is no way to eliminate the hazard, it is advisable to remove that piece of furniture until your child is older.

8. Upholstered furniture should be carefully examined regularly. Children have the capacity to pay infinite attention to detail, and so should you. Look for tacks or staples that may be coming loose. Make sure there are no worn or torn spots that could allow your child to get to the padding underneath. Check buttons to make sure they are good and tight. Look for loose piping, too. Reach down behind the seats or between and under the cushions to make sure that no hazardous things—such as buttons, pencils, or coins—are lurking there.

9. Never allow your child anywhere near exercise machines or any mechanism that is driven with gears, belts, pulleys, or wheels. Even when not in use, these

machines are potentially very hazardous to children. If you have machines of this kind, move them to a part of the house that is off-limits to your child.

10. Watch out for folding or movable furniture. Children are intrigued by things they can make move. So furniture such as deck chairs, reclining chairs and rockers, chairs on casters, captain's chairs, card tables, folding step stools, TV tables, drop-leaf tables, and ironing boards are very dangerous to children because they can pinch or even break tiny fingers. Keep your child away from furniture like this whenever possible, and when it's not possible, keep a very close, vigilant eye on your child.

11. A free-standing partition or decorative screen should be stored away until your child is old enough to understand it isn't a real wall. These items are both pinching and falling hazards.

12. Make sure that you always push dining chairs under the table to discourage your child from climbing up. Avoid using tablecloths, which your child could pull to the floor—along with the table's contents. If you have a low-hanging lamp or chandelier over the table, raise it high enough that your child won't be able to reach it should he happen to maneuver himself to a standing position on the table top. If you have a piano, organ, desk, or personal computer in your home, follow the same rules—keep the bench or chair pushed in and make sure lamps or other potentially hazardous items are not within reach.

Once you have completed this general check, consider the items specific to your home. Whatever they might be, look at your furnishings from a safety standpoint and through the eyes of your small child. When you test, poke, and probe you may be astonished at what you find. Remember the golden rule of child safety: If it's there, your child will find it. If it can be done, your child will do it.

Stairs and Hallways

For your young crawler, climbing the stairs is a thrilling challenge which comes almost naturally. To maneuver back down the stairs is a lot less natural. This learning process requires your careful attention and supervision. For this reason, the most important safety precaution you can take with regard to stairs is to install safety gates at both the top and bottom of each stairway. Remember never to use a pressure gate at the top of the stairs, and if you use a pressure gate at the bottom of the stairs make sure the pressure clamp is to the inside away from your child. Refer to Chapter 6 for more information about the selection and installation of security gates. When installing the gates, consider leaving two or three steps open at the bottom to give your child a "practice" area for climbing.

Other important stairway and hallway tips are:

- Stair and hallway areas should be kept well lit at all times of the day and night. Make sure that light switches are arranged so you can turn lights on or off from either end of the hall and from both the top and bottom of the stairs. The best idea for lighting at bedtime is to install a dimmer on the switch that controls the stair and hallway lights, which will provide much safer lighting than a simple nightlight.
- The safest covering for stairs is wall-to-wall, low-pile carpeting. This will give your child the surest footing and will also provide some cushion in case of a fall. But whatever you use on your stairs, make sure it is slip and trip resistant.
- Make sure that furniture is not placed near stairs where it could be used to climb over the railing or gate in order to gain access to the stairs.
- Check the structural condition of your stairs for loose treads or risers and make sure carpeting is not worn

or coming loose. Watch out especially for loose carpet tacks.

- Open stairs (stairs with open risers) provide one of the greatest safety challenges of all. If the open area of the riser is more than five inches you should install a wooden cross piece on the risers between the stairs or use chicken wire or acrylic panels as a temporary method to keep your child from climbing "through" the stairs. As a safety-conscious parent, remember that it's what works that counts, not how it looks.

- Open balusters on stairs and balconies are another big challenge. If the spacing between the balusters is wider than four inches, a barrier should be installed to prevent the possibility of your child falling through or getting stuck between them. As with open stairs, consider using chicken wire or acrylic sheets that could be attached tightly to the balusters with heavy plastic cable ties. As an easier alternative, there is a product available that was invented by a new father: barriers made of a netted material similar to that used for mesh playpens, and they come in many sizes. Railing nets attach to the rails with ties at the top, bottom and sides, completely covering the open spaces between the balusters.

Railing net

- Make sure your stairways have handrails and check them often to see that they are secure on the wall and not coming loose. Handrails on both sides of the stairs are ideal. Also consider installing extra handrails at a lower level so your toddler can reach them.
- Never place throw rugs at the top of stairs and keep your stairways clear of toys, clothing, and all items that could be tripping hazards. When you are carrying your child up or down the stairs, make sure you can see clearly where you are stepping and always use the handrail. Once your child starts using the stairs, don't allow her to carry sharp or hard objects while climbing or descending them.

TEACHING YOUR CHILD ABOUT STAIRS

Your baby will consider stair climbing an interesting and exciting accomplishment. Work with him closely and teach him how to crawl up and down the stairs safely. To most children, climbing up the stairs comes naturally—but going down is much more difficult. Until he is an accomplished walker, teach him that the safest way down is for him to crawl down backwards on his hands and knees. Once he is ready to start walking down, teach him to always hold on to the handrail. But remember, until you're sure your child has mastered the stairs, keep the safety gates in place and always be there with a helping hand when he is on the stairs.

Laundry Room, Basement, and Sewing Room

These are areas that should be kept strictly off-limits to your child. Install locks or use any of the door safety devices mentioned earlier in this chapter. Even though the door has been secured, there are a number of other precautions to take in the event your child should find her way into these rooms:

- Make sure that all laundry soaps, bleaches, starches, stain removers, fabric softeners, and sprays are placed on a shelf high out of reach or locked safely in a cabinet or cupboard. Dispose of these containers by taking them to the outdoor trash.
- It's best to save your ironing for a time when your toddler is napping. Or make sure she is securely in her playpen where she can't reach the ironing board or the cord to the iron. Remember to keep your iron and ironing board, which could be easily toppled, safely stored away between uses.
- If you have a clothesline, make sure it is high out of your child's reach and wrap up or cut off any excess dangling line.
- Dirty rags or rags with cleaning solutions should be kept out of reach or locked up.
- Never leave water standing in laundry tubs. Empty these tubs immediately after each use.
- Keep scissors, needles, thread, buttons, pins, and all other small or sharp sewing accessories in a locked or latched drawer or cabinet. Your sewing machine should be locked away in a closet or cupboard or, if it has its own cabinet, make sure to shut it away and unplug it after each use.

Household Safety for Every Room

The best way to investigate the safety of your home is to get down to your child's level and take a "crawling tour" of every room on a regular basis. Get down on your hands and knees and look for potential dangers between the floor and about 40 inches above the floor—a yardstick is useful for this. Check the floors, carpets, and rugs for buried dangers like pins, buttons, marbles, paper clips, coins—anything small enough to swallow. Remember to check under furniture, too. Also check walls and woodwork for chipped or peeling paint or plaster. Keep in mind that anything your baby can reach will probably be pushed, pulled, or go into his mouth, so use your imagination.

Here are a few general safety tips that apply to all the rooms in your home:

- Keep your child's toys away from high-traffic areas so that you or other family members don't trip over them.
- Never smoke or drink or carry hot items while carrying or holding your baby.
- Don't allow your toddler to walk or run while eating or carrying anything that could cause injury if she falls.
- Keep pails and pans of water off the floor or keep your child in the playpen or crib when using them. A toddler who falls head first into a pail of water may not have the strength to pull himself out.
- Check all the plants in your home to make sure that none of them are harmful. Even plants that are not poisonous can cause a tummyache if ingested. Remember that hanging plants often drop their leaves to the floor where your baby could easily pick them up. Refer to Chapter 11 and Appendix A for more information about plants.
- Never tie anything, including pacifiers or jewelry, around your baby's neck.
- If you have throw rugs, make sure they all have slip-resistant backings and never use a throw rug or an area rug at the top of a stairway.
- Keep any purses out of your child's reach at all times. Most purses contain many things that are dangerous for children to play with.
- Never place heaters, fans, humidifiers, or other elec-

trical appliances on the floor or anywhere within reach of your infant or toddler.
- At as early an age as possible, teach your child to say her name and address (including the city) and her telephone number (including the area code). Also teach her how to dial the 911 emergency number.

Firearms

If you have firearms in your home, make sure that all the members of your family are trained in safe gun handling and procedures. It's up to you to set a good example. When your child is old enough, you should teach him that firearms are not toys and that "hands off" is the rule. Remember, even if you don't have a gun, about one-fifth of all households do, so your child is likely to encounter a gun at some time.

- All guns should be kept unloaded.
- All guns should be locked up and equipped with trigger locks.
- Ammunition should be locked up in a separate location from firearms.
- Guns and other weapons should be stored out of sight of visitors and be inaccessible to all children.

Emergency Phone List

It's very important that you keep an emergency phone list next to every phone in your home, or at least near one phone on each floor. Make sure the list can be easily read by you, your older children, and any visitors or babysitters.

The list should include the phone numbers for the fire department, police, poison control center, doctor or pediatrician, and the closest emergency hospital or paramedics. Make sure the list also includes your name, address, and phone number, the phone number of a relative if nearby, the phone numbers of a few neighbors, and your and your spouse's work phone numbers, so a visitor or babysitter will have this information if needed.

3

Nursery Safety

Your baby's nursery is a special room . . . her very own, very special place

YOUR BABY'S NURSERY
is a special room. Your child will grow from infant to toddler in what will seem a very short time. And during this progression from crib to youth bed, her room will become her very own special place.

In order to ensure that this room is safe for your infant or toddler, safety should begin at the beginning—with the way you furnish your nursery, the way you use your nursery furnishings and equipment, and a few do's and don'ts that will make safety an everyday practice. Here are three basic steps to follow:

1. Make sure your child's furniture and equipment are *safe*. This is so important to your child's safety that an entire chapter has been devoted to this subject. Please read Chapter 6 carefully for details about how to select safe furnishings and equipment.
2. Use nursery furniture and equipment in the safest possible way and teach the other members of your household and babysitters to do the same.
3. Follow the do's and don'ts listed in this chapter. Become "safety-minded" in your everyday routine and you'll find that the practice of safety will grow as your little one develops.

The Ideal Nursery

It is only natural that most nurseries are equipped well in advance of the arrival of the new occupant. The anticipation of the big event, plus a mind's eye picture of cozy warmth, soft colors, and your new baby's furnishings, makes this an enjoyable project. Being safety-minded in the process will bring added benefits in the days and years to come. Let's take a trip through the ideal nursery from a safety point of view.

JUST OPEN THE DOOR . . .

And while you are opening the door to your new nursery, check to make sure that the handle does not have the type of lock that your child can lock from the inside. It's a simple first step, and one that can save you the worry of being on the outside wanting in.

Many nurseries have closets with sliding or accordion style doors. If yours does, simply equip them as described in Chapter 2.

CHECK THE WINDOWS . . .

The first thing to check when it comes to windows in your nursery is whether or not the windows face east or west. Remember, you'll want to position your baby's crib in a location where the sun cannot shine directly on him, or make sure to keep the drapes or blinds closed when the sun is shining into the room. Even sun streaming through a window can be harmful to your new baby's tender skin.

As your little one approaches the toddler years, you'll want to make sure not to place furniture or toys under a window, which could encourage your child to climb up to it. A few other points about windows in the times of toddlers . . .

- Check the condition of the windows regularly to make sure that the glass is not cracked or broken. Check the screens to see that they are securely in place and that they cannot be pushed out and are not torn.
- Do not rely on a screen to prevent your child from falling through the window. Use window latches, which prevent the window from being opened more than a few inches. There are styles available for the various models of windows. Check the window section in Chapter 2 for more information about window latches.
- If possible, when opening the window make it a practice to open it at the top of the window frame.

SMOKE ALARMS

Many parents feel more comfortable if they have a smoke detector in their child's room. This is a fine idea as extra, added protection for your child, but should be thought of as exactly that—*extra* protection. You should still have smoke and heat detectors placed properly in the halls outside the bedrooms—between your sleeping family and the rest of the house. Please read Chapter 9 on fire safety for more details, or contact your local fire department for free information about smoke and heat detectors.

FIRE IDENTIFICATION STICKERS

Fire identification stickers are highly visible, weather-resistant decals which can be seen clearly day or night to mark the location of your child's room and alert the fire-fighters to clear this area first. "Tot-Finder" stickers are recommended and recognized by all firefighters. Because fire rescuers always enter a burning building on their hands and knees, one should be placed on the outside lower portion of your child's nursery door.

Fire identification sticker

Many fire departments also recommend one to be placed on the outside of the nursery window—but check with your local fire department because there are some areas where this practice is not recommended, or recommended only for windows above the first floor.

Nursery Furnishings and Accessories

With this brief check of the room that will become your "ideal nursery," you're now ready for the furnishings—those special items for your new baby that will add warmth, comfort, and function to make your nursery everything you want it to be.

CRIB AND PLAYPEN SAFETY

In the beginning, the central piece of nursery furniture is the crib. It's the one thing that you will absolutely need, and its selection should be made with safety in mind. Please refer to Chapter 6 for details about selecting a safe crib and playpen for your baby.

Here are a few hints that you should follow for the outfitting and use of your crib and playpen:

- Always check your baby frequently when she's in her crib or playpen.
- If your child is under 4 months old don't leave objects in his crib or playpen that could cause smothering. This includes large stuffed animals or other large toys, heavy blankets, and extra blankets and pillows.
- To protect your baby's head from bumps, fabric-padded bumpers should be used in your newborn's crib and playpen if they do not have soft sides.
- Once your baby is able to pull herself to a standing position, certain things should be removed from her

crib and playpen so she can't use them as stepping stones. These items include padded bumpers, large blankets and pillows, large stuffed animals, and any other large toys.

- Never leave anything hanging over the side of his crib or playpen that he could pull down over himself, such as clothing, diapers, sheets, or blankets.
- Never hang anything on your baby's crib or playpen with strings, ribbons, or cords that are more than 11 inches long. Mobiles should be located where they cannot be reached by your baby.
- Never use a strap or harness device on your child while she is in her crib or playpen.
- Keep his crib and playpen away from drapes, drapery cords, windows, shades and blinds, dresser tops, heaters, fans, lamps, and electrical outlets. In other words, nothing should be within reach of your baby's crib.
- Check often the blankets and bed sheets and their edging for rips and strings.
- Do not use plastic mattress and pillow covers or electric blankets in your baby's crib or playpen.
- When your baby is in her crib, always keep the side rail locked and in the highest raised position.
- Once your baby can pull himself up and stand in his crib, set his crib mattress to the lowest position.
- Use only nonglass, breakproof baby mirrors in your baby's crib or playpen. Attach the mirror to the side rails, or remove the mirror when you are not in the room with your baby.
- Once your baby can sit up on her own, remove any crib gyms or mobiles from both crib and playpen.
- If your child is 35 or more inches tall, he has outgrown the crib and should be sleeping in a regular bed.

The following rules apply to playpens only:

- When your baby is in her playpen, it's best to keep the

playpen in the same room with you or another family member.

- Never leave your baby in or near a mesh playpen which has a drop side in the "down" position.
- If you have a vinyl or fabric playpen, check from time to time to make sure there are no tears that could expose the padding and invite chewing. If you have a mesh playpen, check for tears in the mesh which could cause a hole large enough for tiny hands or feet to be caught.
- Never tie anything across the top of your child's playpen.
- When your child has learned how to climb out of the playpen, it's time to put the playpen away.

THE CHANGING TABLE, AND CHANGING DIAPERS

Make sure your changing table is equipped with a safety strap and use the strap at all times when your baby is on the table. But don't trust the safety strap to protect your baby while you leave the room. Babies can wiggle and slide unexpectedly—so never leave the room while your baby is on the changing table.

If you do not have a changing table, the next best place for changing is in the crib with the side down far enough to allow you to reach over it comfortably. But just as with the changing table, never walk away from the crib when your baby is in it with the side lowered.

Other popular diaper-changing locations, especially when traveling or visiting, are the couch and an adult bed. To give your baby added protection in these locations, create a barrier with pillows or folded blankets or towels placed on either side of the baby to keep him from rolling too far in any direction. If these are not available, the safest place of all is a non-drafty, carpeted area of the floor using a changing pad or towel under your baby to protect both him and the carpet.

All about Diapers. As the oldest of seven children, I can remember my mother mentioning that she could change a diaper in her sleep. Given the quantity of diapers that even one baby uses, I'm sure that you will feel the same way in a very short time. And with a few safety-minded thoughts to keep in mind, the correct way to change diapers will become second nature to you.

You should never leave your baby unattended during the changing process. Remember this when the doorbell or phone rings, or even if you're just going across the room. A big accident takes only a short time, and there is no better prevention than a parent's presence. A few other diaper-changing hints:

- Keep all changing products out of your baby's reach— powder, pins, wipes, oil, etc. Baby powder, talcum powder, and cornstarch can cause respiratory arrest or pneumonia if a large amount is inhaled, so don't let your baby play with the powder containers and never use powders on your baby when you are in front of a fan or breezy window. Wipes and towelettes do not claim to be nontoxic and many contain alcohol, ether, or other undesirable ingredients.
- Though the changing products should be kept out of your baby's reach, they should be within easy reach for you so you do not have to step away from your baby during the changing process. But do not place changing products on shelves over your changing area, where they could inadvertently fall on your baby.
- If you are changing your baby anywhere other than a changing table with a safety strap, make it a practice to keep one hand on your baby at all times.
- Make sure as your baby gets older that the changing table is not located such that your baby is able to "push

off" with her arms or legs from the wall or another piece of furniture.

Diaper Pails. If you use a diaper pail, make sure to keep it tightly closed and out of reach of your child. The cake deodorizers, the liquid used for soaking cloth diapers, and the plastic liners for the pail are all dangerous things and must be kept strictly off-limits. The best advice would be to keep your diaper pail in a locked closet or childproofed cupboard.

NURSERY MONITORS AND INTERCOMS

A nursery monitor or intercom is a good idea if your baby's nursery is not within hearing range of every room in your home. There are many models available, but the most practical are those that offer a portable unit for the parent so you can take the receiver with you from room to room or even to the yard, just as you can with a portable phone. Still, make sure to check on your baby frequently, and if you have a portable monitor, check it every day to make sure the batteries are good.

Nursery monitor

HUMIDIFIERS AND VAPORIZERS

If you use or plan to use a humidifier or vaporizer in your baby's nursery there are a few things you should know about these appliances.

Select a safe, high location for placement of your humidifier or vaporizer, and be sure the cord is not within your child's reach.

Humidifiers and vaporizers should be cleaned frequently and emptied when not in use. If water has been left sitting the appliance should be empied, cleaned, and refilled before use. Recent tests have shown that it is healthier to use distilled water in humidifiers and vaporizers because some water supplies contain chemicals that are unhealthy when they are inhaled in the air.

Many doctors are now recommending cool-mist vaporizers, and the subject of using eucalyptus, menthol, or other medications in vaporizers has become a controversial issue of late. Check with your doctor about which type of vaporizer is best and what is and is not recommended for use in it.

NIGHTLIGHTS

Nightlights are ideal for safely lighting the way in hallways, bathrooms, and your child's room during the night. Here are a few tips on purchasing and using nightlights safely:

- When purchasing a nightlight, check to see that it is certified by Underwriters Laboratories ("UL approved"). If any nightlights you're currently using are not UL approved, get rid of them—an old or poorly made nightlight is a potential hazard.
- Never use a nightlight without the cover that protects the bulb.
- Put nightlights in higher sockets where your infant or

toddler cannot reach them, or install the outlet-cover nightlights that cannot be removed without a screwdriver.

- Never place a nightlight where bedding, draperies, or other materials could hang over it.
- Check your nightlights often and if you detect any scorching or melting, discontinue use of that light immediately.

YOUTH BEDS AND GUARD RAILS

When your child first moves from his crib to a regular bed, you can make it a safe, easy transition by making his bed feel more like a crib. Put the bed in a corner so it is protected by walls at the head and on one side and use a bed guard rail on the other side, leaving the foot of the bed unguarded for your child to use as his exit.

Bed guards have extension legs that fit under the mattress and create a railing-like barrier along the side of the bed to prevent your child from rolling onto the floor.

As an alternative, you could start with the mattress on the floor until your child learns not to roll off—then add the box spring and then the bed frame. As you build the bed to higher levels, try putting cushions or pillows on the floor so that if he does roll off he will have a softer landing.

Once your child has moved to a regular bed, electric blankets are still not recommended—he could wet the bed, pets could scratch the blanket and cause a short, folding the blanket over for long periods could result in overheating, and so on.

While bunk beds may seem appealing from a space-saving standpoint, they are not a good choice for a child's first bed. If you are the parent of twins and prefer bunk beds, it's best to start out with the beds unstacked until you are sure your children are used to the regular bed and each can master the climb to the top bunk. It's important to mention

Bed guard rail

here that, even if you don't have twins, most children love to "trade" beds. So though you may have the top bunk planned for an older child, it is very likely that your toddler will attempt the challenge of that lofty climb.

DRESSERS, DRAWERS, AND OTHER FURNITURE

The innocent-looking furniture in your child's bedroom could be potentially hazardous. Here are a few things to watch out for.

Check the chest of drawers and make sure it is heavy and sturdy enough that it cannot be pulled over by your child. Many children learn this trick: They pull out the bottom drawer and use it as a step stool to reach the top of the dresser. To solve this problem, install a drawer latch in the bottom drawer. If the dresser is of a light weight, also consider purchasing an L-shaped brace from a hardware store and using it to firmly attach the dresser to the wall. Another solution would be to replace the dresser with a heavier, sturdier one.

Check all the drawers in your child's room. Whether the

drawers are in a piece of standing furniture or something built into the wall, make sure that they all have safety stops which will prevent your child from pulling the drawer completely out. If you are in the market for nursery furniture, look for this feature—it will prevent a drawer from falling out and landing on your child. If you find that you have drawers that do not have safety stops, you could install them yourself. But if you're not particularly handy or you're concerned because the piece of furniture is valuable, you may be well advised to consult with a carpenter or furniture maker before attempting this project on your own.

When selecting furniture for your child's room it's best to choose child-sized pieces that are stable, are made of durable materials, and have safe rounded edges and corners.

TOY CHESTS

Toy chests are the best way to avoid clutter in your child's room but there are a few safety tips you should be aware of before buying or allowing your child to use a toy chest.

- If your toy chest has a wooden lid, make sure it has a spring-loaded lid support. The lid support will keep the lid open in any position so that it won't fall and pinch or bang your child's fingers, hands, head, or neck. It will also prevent her from getting trapped inside. If you have a toy chest that does not have a lid support, remove the lid from the chest permanently or until you can have a lid support installed. And make sure that the lid support is the type which will hold its tension without periodical adjustments.
- Check to see that the toy chest has ventilation holes in the front or sides or an air space between the lid and the box. The holes should be positioned so that they cannot be blocked if the chest is pushed against a wall or another piece of furniture.

Spring-loaded lid support (approved by Consumer Product Safety Commission)

- Never put locking or latching devices of any kind on your child's toy chest.
- If you use an alternative storage item, such as a trunk or wicker chest or wooden storage chest, make sure to install a spring-loaded lid support or remove the lid.
- If you are planning to purchase a new toy chest, the safest kinds are those made of a fabric such as canvas or mesh or those made of a high-impact plastic. It is also preferable that it have no lid, or that the lid be extremely light or made of fabric. Make sure it is well ventilated, lightweight, and has no sharp edges or corners.

Sleepwear, Bedding, and Decorative Fabrics

When it comes to sleepwear and bedding, make sure that these items are flame resistant and avoid purchasing any of these products if the labels have been removed. The Consumer Product Safety Commission requires manufacturers to produce only flame resistant sleepwear for children, but daytime wear—such as diapers and underwear—is not required to meet the same standards.

Also make it a point to select only flame resistant materials when purchasing rugs, draperies, and wallpaper for your child's room.

4

Bathroom Safety

Water is magical stuff that appears to come from nowhere, swirls and splashes, and feels good to the
touch

IT SEEMS THAT children
have an endless fascination with water. It's magical stuff
that appears to come from nowhere, swirls and splashes, and
feels good to their touch—so it's only natural that they want
to get into it. Early on, your child will learn that most water

comes from one important place in your home, the bathroom.

Your bathroom is probably the smallest room in your home, yet it's here that many of your child's important early lessons will be learned—bathing, toilet training, toothbrushing, washing hands and face. You and your child will spend much time together here. The exploration of water and the early learning steps of hygiene should be fun for both of you and, by following a few easy steps, it can be safe and secure as well.

Here are the basic rules to keep in mind for a safe and secure bathroom:

1. The only time your infant or toddler should be in the bathroom is when you or another adult are there with him. The bathroom is not a playroom, and an unattended little one can quickly cause danger to himself. Never leave him alone in the bathroom for any reason (even for a few seconds), and take steps now to secure your bathroom door to prevent his entry when unescorted. Door security is covered in Chapter 2.

2. Act now to remove dangerous items from your bathroom or see that they are placed securely beyond the reach of your child. This might sound simple and obvious, but some of the products that can be a threat to your child may surprise you. A list of dangerous products can be found on page 81 of this chapter.

3. Follow safety procedures when using the bathroom and teach your young child and other family members to do the same. The steps outlined here should become second nature to you and your child.

Bathing

Bathing is the number-one indoor water sport for people under 6 years of age. Following these guidelines will help ensure that bathtime rituals, whether for your tiny infant or your splashing, giggling toddler, are the pleasant combination of fun and function they are meant to be.

SAFE BATHING FOR NEWBORNS AND INFANTS

Newborns require sponge baths for the first few weeks until the umbilical cord has fallen off and the area is dry. Your baby should not be placed in water before this.

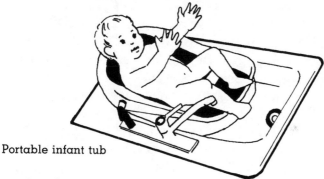

Portable infant tub

Comfort and safety are of primary importance when bathing your newborn. Make sure the room you choose for bathing is warm and draft free. Turn up the heat in winter and turn off the air conditioner in summer. The kitchen sink is preferred by many parents because it is at a comfortable height. Portable infant tubs with an incline are very helpful because they support your baby and leave your hands relatively free for bathing. If you are not using an infant bathtub, place a towel in the sink to keep your baby from sliding around.

Infant Bathing Safety Tips

- Before putting your baby in the tub, test the temperature of the bathwater. A safe temperature range is 90°F to 100°F, 90°–95° being on the cool side and 96°–

100° being ideally warm yet not too hot. While testing with your wrist or elbow is the best self-test method, the safest and most accurate way is to use an unbreakable liquid-crystal bath thermometer.

- Support your baby's head at all times. Use a special infant tub that has this support built in, or carefully hold your baby with one arm while washing with your other hand. Make sure to keep your baby's head well above the water at all times.

- Never add hot water while your baby is in the tub and don't overfill the tub. A couple of inches of water is sufficient.

- To wash your baby, use a very soft washcloth or your hand and a mild soap made especially for a baby's tender skin. Start with your baby's head and face and work your way down. Wash your baby's face with water only, because any soap is too harsh for a young baby's face and may cause skin irritation.

- Wash carefully behind the ears and in all the folds of skin. When washing the genital area, always wash from front to back to avoid bacterial infections. Boys who are uncircumcised should be washed carefully, making sure *not* to pull back the foreskin. This skin will not retract without causing pain until he is 1½ to 3 years old.

- Thoroughly rinse all soap off your baby. Soap left on your baby's skin can cause skin irritation.

- Babies are very slippery when wet! Carefully lift your baby from the tub, placing your hand under your baby's bottom for safe support.

- To prevent your baby from becoming chilled cover her head with the towel, because most body heat escapes from the head. You should gently pat your baby's skin dry—do not rub. Make sure to dry in the folds of her skin, too.

- If you want to take a bath with your baby, follow these safety steps carefully:

Avoid standing in the tub while holding your baby. Fill the tub and check the water temperature. Undress yourself and then your baby. Put a towel on the floor next to the tub and place your baby on the towel. Get into the tub in a seated position, reach over the side of the tub and lift your baby into the tub with you. Seat your baby on your lap with the back of his head resting against your tummy for support while you bathe him. While still sitting, use the towel on the floor to dry your hands, then dry your baby as much as possible.

Place the towel back on the floor, lift your baby out of the tub, and place him on the towel. Now it is safe to stand up and get yourself out of the tub.

SAFE BATHING FOR CRAWLERS AND TODDLERS

It's here that we become even more concerned for safety, because your baby has now developed the ability to move around, with some manual dexterity. In short, she can get into anything, and in the bathroom that spells trouble.

All about Water. The first and most important concern about bathroom water is the temperature of the hot water. The skin of an infant or child burns much more easily than an adult's, and hot liquids, not fire, are the most frequent cause of burns to children. Toddlers are at greatest risk from scalds when they first begin to walk and climb and reach.

- Check the temperature setting of your hot-water heater. If it is above 120°F, lower it to 120°F. (This will still be hot enough for washing dishes and laundry.) Tap water of 150°F can cause a second-degree burn in less than two seconds—yet it takes five minutes for the same burn to occur at 120°F.

■ The temperature-control knobs on hot-water heaters vary from brand to brand. Some have the temperature indicated on the knob and some have "high," "medium," and "low" settings. If the control knob on your water heater does not indicate a precise temperature, use the following procedure: Turn the knob one notch toward the cooler setting. Wait two to three hours and test the temperature of the water by placing a cooking thermometer or bath thermometer in a glass and running hot water over it for a few minutes. If the water is still too hot, repeat the procedure as many times as necessary. Once you have reached the desired temperature, mark your thermostat knob as shown in the illustration. This will help you know if someone accidentally turns the knob to a higher setting.

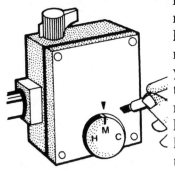

Marking correct
thermostat temperature

■ Always test the temperature of the water before putting your child in the tub: 96°F to 100°F is a safe, comfortable temperature. The most accurate and easiest test is to use a bath thermometer—but if you don't have one, test the water with your elbow or the underside of your wrist and make sure the water feels comfortably warm, not hot. If you are putting your child in the tub while the water is still running, also test the temperature of the water that is coming from the spout.

■ Don't fill the tub too full. If your child is under 6 months, refer to page 71 on infant bathing. If your child is 6 to 12 months old, two or three inches of water is deep enough. As your child grows, the depth of the water can be increased, but it should never be deeper than waist high, seated, for safety's sake.

■ It's not recommended that you continue running the

water after your baby is in the tub, but if you do, always be sure to turn off the hot water first. Even though the tub is filled, the hot water could hurt or startle your child. Also, if you turn the cold water off last, the water spout will not become hot.

- Get into the habit of turning off the hot-water handles as tightly as possible. By the time your child is strong enough to turn them on, you will have taught her the meaning of "hot." Instruct older children not to turn on hot-water taps when their younger sibling is in the tub.

- Never leave bathwater standing in the tub. Instruct all members of your family to drain the tub immediately after bathing.

All about Tubs. The most important rule about the use of the tub: Never take your eyes off your baby while he's in the bathtub and keep at least one hand on him at all times. If the phone or doorbell rings, ignore it or wrap your baby warmly and take him with you. There should be no exception to this rule. If telephone contact is important to you, then consider an answering machine to tell callers "I'm not able to come to the phone right now . . ."

Other important safety tips about the use of the tub:

- Keep washcloth, soap, and other bathing necessities close at hand but out of your baby's reach. There are handy trays made for this purpose that fit over the bathtub.

- Install a shock-absorbent cushion on your tub spout. This will protect your child from bumping her head on the spout, from touching the spout when it's hot, and from being cut on the sharp edges at the opening of the spout. There are many styles of spout covers available and your child will enjoy their fun designs. Just make sure the one you select is thickly cushioned. For a do-it-yourself solution, purchase a one-inch-thick

Do-it-yourself spout cover

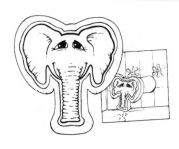

Decorative spout cover

sheet of polyethylene foam at a hardware store, cut it
to size, and secure it to your tub spout with a water-
resistant tape, such as electrical tape.

- Use a rubber bath mat to protect your child against
slips, falls, and a bumped head. Nonskid strips and
appliqués are not recommended because they leave
unprotected areas large enough for tiny feet to slip.
Bath mats are much more comfortable to your baby's
tender bottom. Make sure the rubber bath mat is large
enough to cover the entire bottom of the tub. If you
have a very large tub, you may want to use two mats.

- Teach your child to stay seated while in the tub. When
standing or kneeling in water, children can easily lose
their balance. For children 6 months to 2 years old, a
bathtub sitter is convenient and practical for keeping
your child safely seated. But please remember that
using one does not mean you can leave your child alone
in the tub. As with all safety products, bathtub sitters
are not intended to replace your careful supervision.

- If your tub has glass doors, check to make sure they
are made of safety glass. (Very old homes may not have
safety glass doors.)

Bathtub sitter

- Installing handrails will help your child make safe exits from the tub through all his years of development. Select handrails that are nonslip and have no sharp edges.
- When your child is ready to try washing by herself, put the bar of soap inside a cotton sock and tie the open end. If it's stepped on it won't be as slippery and if she's still in the "everything-in-the-mouth" stage, she'll get the bad taste but won't be able to take a bite out of the soap bar.
- Avoid giving your baby frequent or long bubble baths when between the ages of 6 months and 2 years. Bubble-bath and bath-oil products have ingredients that can strip away your baby's natural skin oil, increasing his chance of developing a rash. These products have also been found to cause urinary tract infections in small children if used too frequently.

The Toilet

Because of your child's natural curiosity about water, the toilet will be the most fascinating contraption she has ever seen! Keep in mind that your child should not learn to be afraid of the toilet because she will soon be ready for toilet training. In the meantime, it is an unsafe and unsanitary place for your child to play and these few basic rules should be followed:

- Install toilet locks on all the toilets in your home. There are several designs available that feature a positive mechanical latching action—this type provides the best measure of safety. Velcro latches are easy to install, but your child will learn to use them faster because they do not require much strength or mechanical ability to open—and since many children's shoes now have Velcro fasteners, children are learning quickly how Velcro works. Velcro latches work best but should be out of your child's reach.

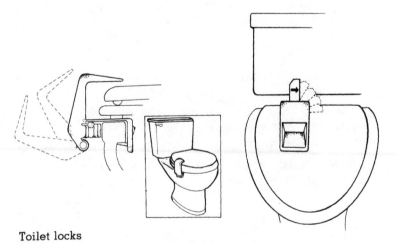

Toilet locks

- Chemicals in automatic toilet bowl cleaners are not safe for children, and the pretty color they turn the water just attracts children more. Even with locks on the bathroom door and on the toilet, stop using automatic toilet bowl cleaners until your child is old enough to know she should not play in the toilet.
- The rule about never leaving your child unattended in the bathroom includes the potty-training stage. This training will require patience on your part, but you must remain in the bathroom with your child while she is on the potty. When your child has graduated to toilet training, make sure you have a toilet trainer with safe, solid, nonskid steps and handrails. There are trainers made now that start out as potty trainers and transform into toilet trainers, and can also be used as step stools. In addition to being safer, they are cost-effective because they serve double and triple duty.

The Sink

While it's important for your child to learn good hygiene at as young an age as possible, don't encourage him to use the sink too soon. Wait until he is tall enough and coordinated enough to be comfortably balanced while standing on a step stool. At the proper time, consider these few simple sink safety tips:

- As with the bathtub, turn off the hot-water handles tightly so your child can't turn them on easily.
- Step stools used at the sink should have trip-proof, nonskid rubber tread. The base of the stool should have nonslip rubber feet.
- Until your child is old enough to use a step stool at the sink, there's an ingenious portable sink you can get that fits over the edge of the bathtub—at just the right height. You could create your own portable sink with

Wait until your child can comfortably stand on a step stool before letting him use the sink

a plastic bowl or plastic washtub set on the lid of the toilet, but be very careful not to tip it.

- Always use paper cups at the bathroom sink because plastics can break and splinter, and because paper cups are sanitary—they are discarded after use and family members will have less chance of passing on cold and flu germs.

Cabinets and Closets

Bathroom cabinets and closets are full of hidden dangers. Here is a list of products typically found in a bathroom that must be removed or locked up:

REMOVE OR LOCK UP THESE BATHROOM PRODUCTS:

Drain cleaner
Scouring powder
Toilet bowl cleaner
Antiseptics
Ointments and salves
Aspirin
Nail polish, polish remover
Artificial nail remover
Rubbing alcohol
Laxatives (including Epsom salts)
Tile cleaner
Disinfectant
Hair treatments (color, permanent, etc.)
All medicines (prescription and nonprescription)
Mouthwash
Hair shampoo and rinse
Hair spray
Bath salts and bath oil
Hair tonics
Deodorizers and air fresheners
Denture cleaner
Perfume, cologne, and aftershave
Cosmetics
Shaving cream
Petroleum jelly
Vitamins and minerals
Aerosol cans
Razors and blades

While some of these products are not toxic if ingested in small amounts, there is no point in taking the chance that your child will ingest only a "small amount."

Remove all potentially harmful products from your bathroom cabinets, including the medicine cabinet, or install cabinet latches. There are specially designed medicine cabinet latches for both hinged and sliding doors. It's better to remove all dangerous products from the cabinet under the sink to a high shelf in a locked closet or to a high, locked cabinet (see Chapter 5 for examples of regular cabinet and drawer latches).

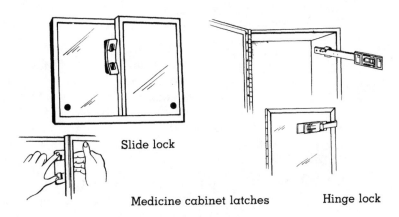

Slide lock

Medicine cabinet latches   Hinge lock

More Bathroom Safety Tips

Even though we have covered tubs, toilets, sinks, and cabinets there are still a few items to keep in mind:

- Make sure that your child cannot lock herself inside the bathroom. This could cause a scare for both you and your child. If your bathroom door has a push-button lock, it should have a small hole on the outside knob. A piece of coat hanger or a large hairpin inserted in the hole will unlock the door. Keep it handy by hanging it out of your child's reach on a nail outside the bathroom door to use should the need arise. If your bathroom door has a key lock, hang the key there.
- Don't allow glass of any kind in the bathroom. Even if it is a product that you do not intend your child to use,

another family member may drop and break the glass container. It is very difficult to clean up broken glass completely. Purchase products with shatterproof containers and, whenever possible, select products with childproof caps.

- Hang hand-washed items above the tub to drip-dry. A wet bathroom floor is very slippery. Clean up other spills of any kind immediately and thoroughly to avoid slips and falls.

- Since the bathroom is the most likely room for slips and falls, you would be wise to install edge and corner cushions to the cabinet tops here. See page 99 for information about these safety items.

- Be very careful about what you put into the bathroom wastebasket. Disposable razors or razor blades, empty containers of cleaning products, empty aerosol cans— all of these dangerous things should be discarded in another place where your child cannot reach them. You may also consider purchasing a lid-locking diaper pail to use as a wastebasket for the bathroom.

- Make sure the rugs you use in the bathroom have non-skid rubber backs. Also choose rugs that are not thick or easy to trip on.

- If you have sliding doors on your tub or a shower stall with a door, you can make these areas off-limits to your

Shower door with Velcro safety strap

child by installing safety latches. We recommend using a Velcro latch and placing it high on the door.

- Electrical appliances should never be used when your child is in the bathroom with you. Many people don't realize that an electrical appliance is dangerous in water even when it's not turned on—it only has to be plugged in. So be sure never to use or place an electrical appliance of any kind near a bathtub, sink, or shower. The safest thing to do is lock them up in a cabinet or closet when they're not in use.

- As with every room in your home your child will be using, make sure you have installed safety covers on all the electrical outlets in this room. Because of water and moisture, the bathroom poses greater electrical hazards. See Chapter 2 for information about the various electrical outlet safety covers that are available.

  If your home was built before 1984, the electrical outlets in your bathroom are probably not equipped with ground fault circuit interrupters (GFCIs). A GFCI senses leaks in the current and breaks the circuit immediately, preventing electrical shock. One GFCI unit can handle several outlets when installed correctly by your electrician.

You and your baby will spend much time in the bathroom together, and if you have made this room as safe as it can be, the time you spend together here will be as rewarding as possible.

5

Kitchen Safety

Some toddlers can remember their first kitchen experience—playing with a wooden spoon and small metal pan

BY THE AGE of two, most self-respecting little ones have learned what the kitchen is— it's the place where food is prepared. As such, it contains a fascinating array of gadgets and devices: A big box keeps things cold; another box warms food for meals; something makes a funny noise and cleans plates and cups for use another day.

Some toddlers can even remember their first kitchen experience—sitting in the high chair and being handed a wooden spoon and a small metal pan. Too uncoordinated at first to hit the pan on the first try, the basis for kitchen curiosity has been established nonetheless.

Most kitchens are the hub of family activity so it's likely your baby will spend more waking hours here than in any other room in your home. This exposure, the endless array of potential dangers, and the desire to be a little helper mean that your kitchen will require the most attention when it comes to childproofing and safety practices. Fortunately, many practical devices have been designed to aid you—and combined with sound, sensible safety practices, this room will be a safer place for your child.

The Stove and Oven

Of all household devices, the stove and oven are at the top of the list of safety concerns of parents of toddlers. If your little one is even fairly active, the image of your child on a small stool pulled up to the stove to "do some cooking" is enough to strike fear in the hearts of even the most sturdy of us.

The stove is one of the things in your home that should be made strictly out-of-bounds to your child. Start early to teach your child the stove is a "no-no" whether it is on or off. The importance of teaching your child the word "hot" cannot be overemphasized, and one or two supervised demonstrations will likely be enough.

But it doesn't stop there. Here are a number of useful tips and devices that apply directly to the stove and oven and their safe use:

- Use the back burners whenever possible, especially for frying and boiling. If you must use the front burners, turn the pot handles toward the back of the stove (but not over another hot burner). This will remove your child's temptation to test his reach, and it will also prevent handles from being caught on clothing or being tipped by you or another family member passing by the stove.

- Most stoves have the knobs located quite logically for the convenience of the user so, of course, they are easy to use. Modern stoves emphasize the fact that the burners heat up quickly and achieve red-hot cooking temperatures in a minute or so.

- Stove knob covers are specifically designed to prevent your child from turning on the stove or oven. These fit both gas and electric stoves and work effectively until your child has developed considerable strength and dexterity—and by that time you will have taught her the dangers. Just make sure you replace the covers after each use and never allow your child to see how they work. Another option is to remove the knobs altogether when you are not using the stove.

- When the stove is in use, tiny little fingers must be kept away from hot pots and burners. Special stove guards are available for this purpose and are also helpful in reminding you to keep your pot handles turned inward. The best stove guards are those designed like a small fence that wrap around the top of the stove at the outside edges and adhere to the top with rubber suction cups. Make sure the one you select wraps all the way around the sides of the stove because this style not only guards the burners from the side, but also has more suction cups and is therefore more secure should your child grab the bars.

- Even though your oven may be well insulated, the door can become very warm when the oven is on. Remember

Remove stove knobs

or install stove knob covers

Stove guard

that "very warm" to an adult is "hot" to a small child's delicate skin. Make sure your child is not within reach of the oven when it is on.

- Never use the cupboards over the stove to store cookies, candy, or other things your child may attempt to climb up to reach.
- Don't hold your child or allow others to hold your child

while standing near the hot stove or other hot appliances.

- When you are cooking greasy foods that have a tendency to splatter or pop, use a splatter screen over the pan or keep the lid on, and make sure your child is nowhere near the stove.

Appliance Safety in General

The general rule of appliance safety is that the appliance is for adult use only. Here again, there are a number of helpful devices and worthy tips to minimize the risks involved.

Dishwashers, ovens, and microwaves can be secured with fairly simple appliance latches. These two-piece latches attach easily, via adhesive backs, to the sides or tops of your appliances. Even if you are using this type of safety latch, be sure to follow the other safety practices in this chapter regarding the use of dishwashers, ovens, and microwaves.

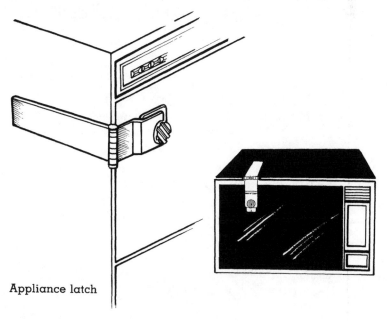

Appliance latch

In addition to the appliance latch, it's also best to locate your microwave where your child cannot reach the controls. If this is not possible, unplug it when it is not in use and make sure the electrical outlet is equipped with a safety cover.

Your dishwasher holds many items that your child should not reach—knives and other sharp cooking utensils, glassware, and so on. To make doubly sure your child is safe, use the appliance latch mentioned above and follow these safety practices:

- Always keep your dishwasher's closing latch in the locked position.
- Store knives and other sharp utensils with the sharp edges pointing down into the silverware basket.
- Store the larger sharp cooking utensils (such as cheese graters or food processor blades) at the back of the top rack.
- Wait to put the soap in the dishwasher until just before you run it.
- Never walk away from your dishwasher while the door is open.

While the refrigerator is a major kitchen appliance, it can be secured fairly easily. You can prevent your child from opening the refrigerator door by installing a refrigerator latch at the top of the door out of his reach. There are several types available, but those made of Velcro are sure to fit all styles of refrigerators. As with all safety devices, don't allow your child to see how it works. By the time he is able to figure it out for himself, you will have taught him that the refrigerator is off-limits. Remember, though, even if you have installed a safety latch on your refrigerator, remove all dangerous items such as vitamins and medicines or put them in a locked or hard-to-open box, and make sure you frequently discard spoiled or unwanted foods.

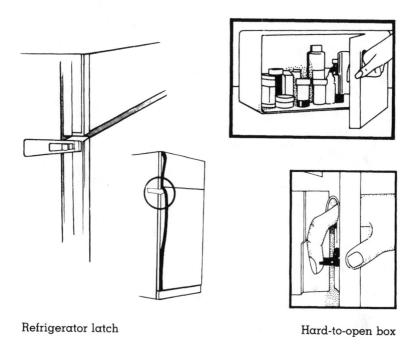

Refrigerator latch   Hard-to-open box

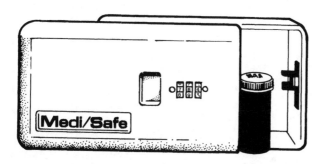

Safe box with combination lock

If you use refrigerator magnets, put them away for a few years. These magnets can easily come loose and drop to the floor where your baby would be sure to find them.

Here are a few additional appliance tips, just for safety's sake:

- If you have a trash compactor, make sure it will not operate when the door is open and that it can only be turned on with a key, which should be kept well hidden.
- If your garbage disposal works by a switch on the wall or counter, you should install a safety lock switch to keep your child from turning it on. With this special switch your garbage disposal cannot be turned on without the key. This device is fairly simple to install and is well worth the effort.
- If you have a separate deep freezer, keep it locked and the key hidden.
- Always push your small appliances—such as toasters, coffee makers, and food processors—to the back of the counter and never let their cords lay near the edge or dangle over the edge of the counter. Also make sure to keep them unplugged when not in use and see that the electrical outlets near them are installed with safety covers.

Safe Storage

Not only does the kitchen hold a vast selection of appliances, but it is also the major storage area of potentially harmful items in your home. The following is a list of items frequently found in the kitchen that should always be kept in locked or latched cabinets or drawers:

ALWAYS KEEP THESE KITCHEN ITEMS LOCKED UP:

Knives	Silverware
Cooking utensils	All glassware
Food processor blades	Can opener
Plastic bags	Scissors
Plastic wrap	Vegetable peeler
Foil wrap	Trash bags
Graters and slicers	Batteries
Coins and buttons	Hard candy
Nutcracker and pick	Gum
Corkscrew and corks	Tools
Aerosol products	Breakable dishes
Rubber bands	Small appliances
Heavy pots and utensils	Pencils
Marbles	Pet food

While some of these items may not be present in your kitchen, check the contents of your cabinets and drawers carefully—you may find other potentially harmful items not listed here. Refer to Appendix B for a more comprehensive list of harmful products.

To protect your child from those items stored in cabinets, it's best to use cabinet latches. These latches are inexpensive and easy to install—and they provide good protection against your toddler's normal curiosity.

For potentially harmful items stored in drawers, drawer latches are available and, again, they are inexpensive and fairly easy to install. Always remember to push drawers closed so that the latches are activated. Drawers without safety latches should be closed tightly, too, to avoid bumped heads. Also check all the drawers to make sure each one has a safety catch which will prevent it from being pulled out and falling to the floor.

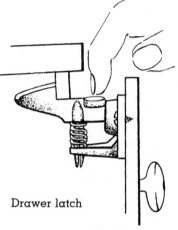

Drawer latch

Other locking options that may be appropriate for the broom closet, pantry, and so on are discussed in the door safety section of Chapter 2. Please refer to that section for details.

With regard to the harmful products sometimes found in the kitchen, the best advice is to move them. It is essential that you remove the household products that are normally stored in the under-the-sink area. If you don't really need them, get rid of them. If you do, move these products to a high place and make sure that the cabinet or closet is locked at all times. When purchasing new products, double the safety by choosing those with childproof caps.

The following is a list of dangerous household products typically found in the kitchen:

KEEP THESE OUT OF REACH AS WELL:

Ammonia	Lighter fluid
Lye	Medicines
Vitamins	Furniture polish
Shoe polish	Window cleaner
Alcohol	Waxes
Scouring powder	Cleaning solutions
Detergents	Aerosol cans
Pesticides	Rug cleaner
Drain cleaner	Mothballs, flakes
All soaps	Oven cleaner
Metal polish	Candles
Rust remover	Glue and paste
Matches	Fabric softener
Bleach	Dishwasher soap
Plant food	Plant sprays
Air fresheners	Toothpicks
Spot cleaner	Dry-cleaning fluid
Alcoholic beverages	Meat tenderizer
Vinegar	Seasoning salts
Flavoring extracts	Cooking wine
Dried beans and peas	Popcorn

You may, at first glance, tend to question whether some of the items listed above are really "dangerous products." Popcorn, for example. Well, dried beans, peas, and popcorn are choking hazards. Toothpicks are common, but they can pierce an eye or eardrum or can cause suffocation if swallowed. Small items are best put away for safety's sake.

Never put a toxic substance in an empty food or drink container; someone could drink it by mistake. Always keep these things in their original containers with the labels intact.

And one other word of advice—even though you have taken every precaution to lock away dangerous products, prepare yourself ahead of time so that in the event any of these is swallowed by your child, you know exactly what to do. Refer to Chapter 11 for details on this subject.

Cooking and Dining Safety

Once the kitchen has been secured with attention to the stove, oven, appliances, and storage areas, proper safety practices must be followed while you are cooking and dining. No matter how many safety devices are installed in the kitchen, nothing is more frightful than the image of an infant under foot when someone is lifting a pot of boiling potatoes from the stove, or a toddler's little hand reaching for a carving knife that was left carelessly at the edge of the countertop.

When you're cooking, keep these tips in mind so your cooking practices will be as safe as your recently childproofed kitchen:

- If your infant or toddler is in the kitchen with you while you are cooking, make sure she is in a safety seat, high chair, or playpen so that she is out of reach of the stove, oven, or other hazards. Children too old for high chairs or playpens should not be allowed to play underfoot in the kitchen while you're cooking.
- Never leave knives out on the counter while you're cooking—put them into the locked drawer as soon as you are finished using them. If you have a magnetic knife holder, stop using it and keep your knives locked up instead. Most childhood knife accidents happen when the adult using the knife is distracted or hurried.
- While you are cooking, make it a habit to push other cooking utensils such as meat forks, hand mixers, etc.,

Children should not be underfoot while you're cooking

to the back of the counter where they are out of reach of tiny hands.

- Don't leave hot pans and casserole dishes, adult food, or alcoholic drinks on a table within reach of your baby or in a place which your baby can reach by climbing.
- Due to the risk of suffocation, plastic grocery bags should be thrown out or put out of reach and locked up. Tie knots in dry-cleaning bags and throw them away immediately. Discard used plastic wrap immediately and keep boxes of plastic wrap and plastic bags locked up. Any boxes of foil or plastic wrap that have jagged cutting edges can cause nasty cuts—so keep these locked up, too.
- Install a smoke alarm and equip your kitchen with a fire extinguisher for stove-top fires and other emergencies in or near your kitchen. See Chapter 9 for detailed information about smoke alarms and fire extinguishers.
- After opening glass baby food jars, examine the jars for chips in the glass. If you discover any chips, throw

Always keep a fire extinguisher in the kitchen

away that jar, food and all. Do not feed your baby from that jar.

- Always be careful to test the temperature of the food you are giving to your child. Be extra careful with microwaved food or drinks. Because microwaves do not heat evenly, the container may not feel hot even when the food or drink is scalding. After heating your baby's bottle, shake it well and test the temperature on the inside of your wrist. If you have heated food for your baby, stir it well and check the temperature carefully.
- Make sure all of your child's drinking bottles, cups, and dishes are made of unbreakable plastic or paper.
- Wastebaskets are an irresistible temptation to crawlers and toddlers. Make sure your wastebasket has a lid that cannot be removed by your child, or lock it up in a cabinet, closet, or pantry. Take extra precautions when throwing things away. Put such things as sharp can lids and razor blades inside a box or wrap them in

something and discard them in your outdoor trash where your child won't get to them.

- Once your baby starts climbing, don't leave your step stool out in the kitchen. Lock it away in a closet or pantry.
- If the countertops in your kitchen have sharp edges and corners you should install corner guards and edge cushions to protect your child against serious injury from an accidental bump or fall.

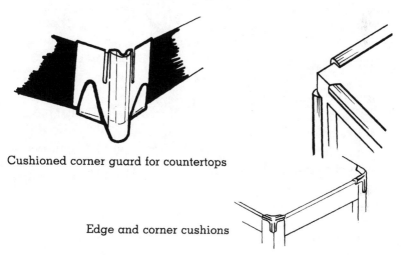

Cushioned corner guard for countertops

Edge and corner cushions

Mop spills from the floor immediately—before your child has a chance to slip. Clean up any broken glass by wiping with a wet paper towel and then vacuuming thoroughly so there is less chance of leaving any glass splinters behind.

- As with every room in your home, make sure you have installed safety covers on all the electrical outlets in the kitchen. See Chapter 2 for information about the different designs available.
- Hard or round foods such as nuts, popcorn, chewing gum, grapes, round pieces of hot dog, raisins, hard candies, and round pieces of raw carrots are very dangerous and can be deadly to children under 4 years of

age. Ask your doctor when your child is old enough to eat these foods.

- Do not give honey to your infant if he is under 1 year old. Honey has been linked to a form of botulism that affects only infants.

Rules for safe dining apply to that age when your baby can sit unassisted in a high chair, at a feeding table, or in a hook-on chair. Always make sure that the seat has a safety belt with a crotch strap, and that you always use it. Position the seat away from counters, tables, stove, oven—any location where your baby could grab at things she shouldn't touch. Even then, it's always best never to leave your baby unattended in the chair.

In your dining area make it a habit to push dining chairs under the table. This will discourage your child from trying to climb onto the chairs and then onto the table or counter. Rubber caps on the bottoms of chair legs will keep the chairs from sliding easily if your baby tries to pull the chair out for himself.

Remember that drop-leaf tables can pinch your baby's fingers and bump heads. Position the table so the leaves cannot be moved and the leaf supports cannot be played with.

Dangling tablecloths seem to invite children to pull on them, bringing the contents of the table to the floor. Remove your tablecloths and instead use placemats that won't slide easily if your baby grabs for them.

Dining-area seating for your baby is frequently the traditional high chair or a "hook-on" chair, followed by the booster seat as she grows. Safety information on these chairs and seats is contained in detail in Chapter 6, and should be studied so that you can make the safest and best selection for your baby.

The following are tips for the safe use of chairs in the dining area.

SAFETY TIPS FOR HIGH CHAIRS

- Place your baby's high chair so his feet and hands cannot reach the table, cabinets, or other furniture that could be used to push off from.
- When attaching the tray to the high chair, make sure your baby's fingers are safely out of the way.
- Always make sure you have firmly locked the high-chair tray in place.
- Don't allow your child to attempt to climb into the high chair unassisted.
- Don't allow older children to climb on or hang on to the high chair when your baby is in it.
- Never allow your child to stand in her high chair. Use the safety belt to discourage this.

SAFETY TIPS FOR HOOK-ON CHAIRS

- Make sure your hook-on chair has safety clamps or locks for the underside of the table so the chair cannot be wiggled loose, and always make sure these clamps or locks are firmly in place before seating your child in the chair.
- Never use a hook-on chair on a glass table, pedestal table, loose-top table, card table, on the leaf of a table, or on any table your child is able to rock.
- Never place a dining chair under your child's hook-on chair because he may try to stand on the dining chair or use it to push his hook-on chair off the table.
- Don't allow other children or pets under or near a hook-on chair when your baby is in it. They could cause the chair to lift up and off the table.
- Always remove your baby from the chair before releasing the locks or clamps.
- Discontinue using a hook-on chair if your child is ca-

pable of bouncing or moving the chair up and down while sitting in it, your chair has a snap-together design and your child is capable of unsnapping parts of it, or your child weighs 30 pounds or more.

SAFETY TIPS FOR BOOSTER SEATS

- Your child's booster seat should have a safety belt to attach the seat firmly to the chair. If it doesn't, use the seat in a chair with arms to prevent the booster seat from slipping off the chair.
- Make sure the seat is at a comfortable height for your child. Some seats have more than one level so that the height can be adjusted as your child grows.

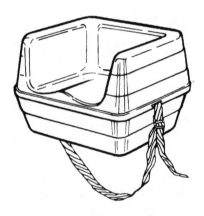

Booster seat with safety strap

II

Safety in Your Home

6

Selecting Safe Baby Furniture and Equipment

It's important to realize that your baby will develop quickly and the investment you make today must be correct for tomorrow

WHEN THERE IS a first-born on the way, the process of selecting baby furniture and equipment appropriately begins well ahead of the new arrival; your new baby will need a car seat for that first car trip home from the hospital and his well-equipped nursery should be ready when he arrives. If this is your first-born, safety may not be the first thing on your mind. But it's important to realize that your baby will develop quickly and the investment you make today in furniture and equipment must be right for tomorrow, when you'll be concentrating on safety as well as durability, attractiveness and value.

This chapter covers the safety features you should look for when selecting furniture or equipment for your child. There are three important general rules to follow concerning your child's furniture and equipment:

1. The Juvenile Products Manufacturers Association (JPMA) sponsors a voluntary certification program to assure parents that certain high chairs, playpens, carriages, strollers, walkers, and gates meet safety standards. To earn the JPMA seal, manufacturers must submit their products to a yearly examination by a testing laboratory. Look for the JPMA seal when purchasing products for your children's use.

Seal of the Juvenile Products
Manufacturers Association

2. Don't buy a product that does not include complete instructions. Make sure the product is right for your child's age, size, and development. Carefully follow the manufactuers' instructions for assembly and use. If the item you purchase requires assembly, have someone double-check your work before allowing your child to use it.

3. Purchasing a safe product isn't enough. It must be used correctly in order to provide the maximum safety for your child. For tips about using these products safely, refer to the chapters listed below with each product.

Carriages and Strollers

Look for the JPMA seal and the following features:

- A wide wheel base and large wheels to prevent tipping.
- It must be properly balanced for stability on inclines.
- If the stroller has a reclining seat, make sure it can't tip backward when your baby lies down.
- No exposed coil springs or any other moving parts that can pinch.
- It must have a latching device that will prevent the stroller or carriage from folding accidentally. If it has a canopy, this should lock securely, too.
- The brakes should be easy to use and very effective. A two-wheel braking system is much safer than a one-wheel brake. The brakes must be out of your child's reach while she's in the stroller or carriage so that she cannot disengage them herself.
- It must have seat belts that are securely attached to the frame and easy to use. Make sure the belts fit snugly around your child and stay fastened.
- If the stroller has a shopping-basket feature, it must be located low on the back and directly over or in front of the rear wheels.

Refer to Chapter 14 to learn about the safe use of strollers and carriages.

Changing Tables

Look for these important features:

- Safety straps to prevent your child from rolling around or off the table.
- Drawers or shelves that are easily accessible without leaving your baby unattended. It's best that the shelves be enclosed with doors to prevent your child's access to the supplies.
- Safety stops on the drawers to prevent the drawers from being pulled all the way out.
- Safety latches on the drawers and doors so your child will not have access to the contents when he starts toddling around. The best models have this extra safety feature.

Refer to Chapter 3 to learn about the safe use of changing tables.

Child Carrier Seats and Infant Seats

When shopping for a child carrier or infant seat look for the following safety features:

- Make sure it has a wide, sturdy base for extra stability.
- The carrier should have a nonskid bottom or nonskid feet to prevent slipping.
- Make sure the supporting devices and frames are sturdy and lock securely.
- The seat must have safety belts for both waist and crotch and the buckle should stay firmly locked but be easy to use.

Safety warning: Never purchase a child carrier or infant seat for use as a car seat.

Refer to Chapter 14 to learn about the safe use of infant seats and child carriers.

Backpack and Sling-Style Child Carriers

When selecting a backpack or sling-style carrier, look for these features:

- Make sure it fits your baby properly. Check to see that it has enough depth to support your baby's back. Make sure the leg openings are small enough to prevent your baby from slipping out, yet big enough to avoid chafing her legs.
- Make sure the straps are wide or padded so they won't dig into your shoulders.
- Look for sturdy materials with strong stitching or large, heavy-duty snaps to prevent your baby from falling out.
- The safest backpack carriers have a padded covering over the metal frame near your baby's face to protect your baby from bumps.
- Test the carrier to make sure you can put it on and take it off without assistance.
- Restraining straps are essential for backpack carriers. Make sure they are sturdy and easy to use.
- Check to see that the frames on backpack carriers have no pinch points in the folding mechanism.

Safety Warning: Never use a back carrier before your baby is 4 to 5 months old and his neck is strong enough to withstand jolts. Sling-style carriers should be designed to provide head and neck support for your baby if he is under 4 or 5 months old.

Refer to Chapter 14 to learn about the safe use of backpack and sling-style carriers.

Cradles and Bassinets

Check to see that the cradle or bassinet you select has these safety features:

- Make sure it has a sturdy bottom and a wide, stable base.
- Read the manufacturer's guidelines on the appropriate weight and size of babies who can safely use the bassinet or cradle.
- See that it has smooth surfaces—no protruding staples or other hardware that could hurt your baby.
- The legs must be strong and stable.
- If the cradle or bassinet has legs that fold for storage, make sure that it also has effective locks so that the legs do not accidentally fold while in use.

Cribs and Mattresses

When selecting a crib and mattress, look for a label that says they meet the standards set by the Consumer Product Safety Commission and make sure they have the following safety features:

- The slats of the crib should be spaced no more than 2⅜ inches apart. The slats should be sturdy and firmly attached. There should be no crossbars on the sides.
- Corner posts must not extend any higher than ⅝ of an inch to prevent entanglement of clothing.
- There should be no cutouts in the headboard or footboard and the panels should be made of a material which will not splinter.
- The mattress must fit snugly. You should not be able to fit more than two fingers between any one side of the mattress and the side of the crib. (The mattress

edges must fit tightly against the other 3 sides of the crib.)

- Make sure the mattress support is securely attached to the headboard and footboard.
- The drop-side release latches should not be reachable by your child in the crib or, if they are, the latches must have a safety device to prevent your child from releasing them herself.
- Make sure the drop-side latches securely hold the sides in the raised position.
- The drop sides, when lowered, should be at least 4 inches above the mattress. The minimum side-rail height should be 22 inches from the top of the railing to the mattress when it is set at the lowest position.
- Check to make sure none of the screws or bolts is missing and that all are secure and tight. Check the glued joints also to make sure they are secure.
- When you buy bumper pads for the crib, make sure that they fit around the entire crib, that they tie or snap into place, and that they have at least six straps.
- Portable mesh cribs should not have holes large enough to allow your baby to poke his fingers through or to catch his buttons.

Safety Warning: When your child reaches 35 inches in height or can climb or pivot over the sides, the crib should be replaced with a bed.

Avoid using old or hand-me-down cribs. While they may have antique or sentimental value, few can pass all the requirements necessary to ensure your child's safety. If money is a problem and you cannot avoid using an older crib, check it very carefully against the above list before allowing your child to use it.

Refer to Chapter 3 to learn about the safe use of cribs and mattresses.

Walkers

Look for the JPMA seal and watch for these safety features:

- The walker should be stable enough that it cannot tip over if your child leans to one side or attempts to pick up a toy. Make sure the wheel base is wider and longer than the seating area. This will give the walker more stability and reduce the chance of tipping.
- Select a walker with wheels that are sturdy and ride smoothly.
- If the walker has coil springs, there must be plastic sleeves over these for protection.
- Check all the metal and plastic parts to be sure there are no sharp edges or points.
- If you select an X-frame type of walker, it should have a protective shield on the X-joint to prevent finger entrapment.
- Check the locking devices to make sure they are strong and secure enough not to collapse during use.

Security Gates

What to watch for when selecting a security gate:

- Under no circumstances should accordion-style gates be used. The Consumer Product Safety Commission warns against these expandable gates with V-shaped or diamond-shaped openings along the top edge. Children can be pinched or become trapped by this type of gate.
- Select a gate with a straight top edge. Make sure it has a rigid mesh or plastic screen or has narrowly spaced metal or wooden slats.

- Check pressure-bar gates to make sure they are strong enough to resist forces exerted by your child. Do not select a pressure gate for use at the top of stairs.

Refer to Chapter 2 to learn about the safe use of security gates.

High Chairs and Hook-On Chairs

Look for the JPMA seal and watch for these safety features:

- The chair should have a strong frame, strong joints, and a strong seat so that it can withstand rough treatment.
- A high chair should have a wide base for good balance and stability.
- Make sure it has a strong restraining device to keep your baby secured in the chair seat. This device should include a crotch strap, be independent of the tray, and be easy to fasten and unfasten.
- Test the high-chair tray to see that it stays in position once it is properly locked.
- Watch out for holes or openings that could catch fingers, toes, or buttons.
- The chair should have an easy-to-clean finish that won't peel, bubble, or splinter.
- If it is a folding high chair, it must have a secure locking device to prevent it from collapsing accidentally.
- A hook-on chair should have a clamp that locks to the table for added security.
- If the chair is made with tubing, check the caps or plugs at the ends of the tubing to make sure they are firmly attached and cannot be pulled off by your child.

Refer to Chapter 5 to learn about the safe use of high chairs and hook-on chairs.

Playpens

When selecting a playpen or play yard, look for the JPMA seal and for these safety features:

- If the playpen is made with mesh, the holes in the mesh netting should be small enough—no larger than ¼ inch in diameter—so that buttons, fingers, or toes cannot be caught.
- Check to see that the mesh is securely attached to the top rail and to the floor plate. Inspect the vinyl to make sure it is strong and thick enough to survive your baby's teething and chewing stage.
- The legs and frame must be stable and sturdy.
- The playpen should have a comfortable, well-fitting foam pad.
- Make sure the sides are at least 20 inches high to discourage your child from attempting to climb out.
- If staples are used in the construction of the playpen, make sure they are firmly installed and none is missing or loose.
- A wooden playpen should have slats no more than 2⅜ inches apart. Check to see that the slats are secure and strong.
- Check to make sure no screws or bolts are missing and that all are secure and tight. Check the glued joints also to make sure they are secure.

Safety Warning: The Consumer Product Safety Commission warns that you should never leave your infant in a mesh playpen or portable crib with the drop side down because there is a trapping hazard in the loose mesh. Even when your child is not in the playpen, it's recommended that you don't leave the drop side down.

Refer to Chapter 3 to learn about the safe use of playpens.

7

Playing It Safe with Toys

You'll be amazed at how delighted your little one is
with the simplest of things around her

PLAYTIME IS A perfectly
natural activity for every child at any age. Even at the infant
stage, your little one will amaze everybody at the delightful
time she can have with even the simplest of things around
her.

Grandparents, aunts and uncles, and friends will want to enhance your infant's pleasures with a toy of their selection . . . a toy that they think is cute. Bright colors, interesting designs, even familiar cartoon characters mean to most adults that a fine addition to your little one's toy collection is in the offing.

Without wishing to be critical of this inevitability, there are underlying safety considerations that the generous benefactor may not have considered.

While play provides many opportunitites for your child to learn and grow mentally, socially, and physically, there are four key points to selecting the right toys for your child. The perfect toy should be:

1. Interesting and appealing to your child
2. Suited to your child's mental and social development
3. Compatible with your child's physical capabilities
4. Well constructed, durable, and safe

The last three points on this list have everything to do with how safe a toy will be for your child.

Don't assume that the construction of the toy is the only factor in making a toy safe. Each toy must also be suited to your child's age and ability level. Always look for age recommendations on toys. Some toys are recommended for older children simply because they may be hazardous in the hands of a younger child. Never select a toy that does not have an age label and never assume that the age label is accurate—check the toy carefully before allowing your child to play with it.

It's not safe to give your child a toy intended for an older child thinking that it will be a good challenge for him or that he will "grow into it." Toys can be dangerous if they are not related to the age level of your child. For example, a toy that has many small removable parts may be perfect for a 6-year-old, but a crawling infant may swallow those small parts. And there are tools that may be skillfully handled by a 12-

year-old that could cause injury to her little brother. Remember to keep all toys designed for your older children out of the little one's reach and teach your older children to keep their toys away from their younger siblings.

So, as you choose your child's toys, keep in mind your child's age, interests, and skill level and look for quality design and construction in all toys you purchase. Make sure that all instructions are clear. Look for safety labels such as "flame retardant/flame resistant" on fabric products; "UL approved" on electrical items; and "washable/hygienic materials" on stuffed toys and dolls.

Under 3 Years Old

SMALL PARTS

If your child is under 3 years old, the big things to watch out for are the small things—any pieces or parts of a toy small enough to swallow. Look for parts that could fall off, break off, or be pulled off—such as buttons, glass or plastic eyes or beads, removable squeakers on squeeze toys, small batteries, marbles, and coins. Also watch for things that can be compressed to a size small enough to fit into your child's mouth, especially certain squeeze toys, teethers, and paci-

 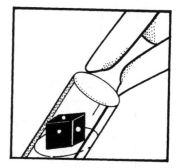

Small Objects Tester, designed by the Consumer
Product Safety Commisson

fiers. The Consumer Product Safety Commission has designed a Small Objects Tester that you can use to see if an object is potentially dangerous because of its size. If an object fits entirely within this cylinder, it fails the CPSC test because it is considered small enough to be a choking hazard. Even though the law bans small parts in new toys intended for children under 3 years of age, you should not assume that every toy has been properly tested.

CORDS AND STRINGS

Another important thing to watch out for if your child is under 3 is any toy with strings longer than 12 inches. You should never hang toys with long strings, cords, loops, or ribbons in cribs or playpens or around your child's neck or wrist because your child could become entangled. If you have a crib gym, make sure to remove it from the crib once your child can pull up on his hands and knees.

PACIFIERS, TEETHERS, AND RATTLES

You should give very special attention to your baby's pacifiers, teethers, and rattles.

When selecting a pacifier, make sure the guard shield is large enough that it will not fit in your baby's mouth. The small pacifiers that newborns use are quickly outgrown, so check the sizing of your child's pacifier often. Make sure that the guard shield is flexible and has ventilation holes. These holes make breathing possible should your baby get the pacifier shield into her mouth and the flexiblity of the shield will make it easier to remove. The nipples of a pacifier can deteriorate with age and use, so you should check often for holes and tears that could cause the nipple to break off in your baby's mouth. Never make a do-it-yourself pacifier using a baby bottle nipple.

Never hang a pacifier on a ribbon or string around your baby's neck and don't pin the pacifier to his clothing. If you're tired of playing the pacifier pickup game with your child, there are special pacifier holders with safety clasps for this purpose.

When selecting rattles and teethers for your baby, make sure they are virtually indestructible. Babies love to bang things, so rattles must be durable. Teethers and rattles should have handles larger than two inches in diameter so that they cannot be lodged in a baby's throat. Remember always to remove teethers and rattles from your baby's crib or playpen when your baby is asleep.

Under 7 Years Old

If your child is under 7 years old, all toys should be free of sharp glass or metal edges and should not have any parts with the potential of breaking and exposing sharp edges.

Your child under 7 should *not* be exposed to the following kinds of toys:

- Electrically operated toys with heating elements or motors with electrical or moving parts that are not enclosed and secured.
- Shooting games or shooting toys such as air rifles, arrows or darts, dart guns, guided missiles, or remote-control airplanes.
- Painting sets, chemistry sets, or model rocket and airplane sets that contain toxic chemicals.
- Ill-balanced tricycles or wagons that may topple.
- Flammable costumes.
- Junior carpentry or woodworking sets.
- Any toy that could shatter or break as a result of rough use or abuse, leaving sharp edges or points.

Beware of Balloons

According to the Consumer Product Safety Commission, inhaling an uninflated balloon or pieces of a broken balloon is one of the leading causes of suffocation death of children. A small child can accidentally suck a balloon down her throat while trying to blow it up. Some children think it's fun to chew on a piece of balloon or to stretch it across their mouth and suck in or blow bubbles, but the balloon can easily be sucked into the airway. And because balloons mold to the contours of the throat and adhere there, they can quickly cause suffocation. Carefully follow these safety rules concerning balloons:

- Do not allow your child under 6 years old to blow up a balloon. Always blow it up for him.
- Always supervise children under 6 years old when they are playing with balloons.
- When your child is old enough to understand, warn her of the danger of sucking or chewing on balloons.
- Keep balloons safely out of reach when it's not planned playtime and be sure to pick up and safely dispose of all the pieces of broken balloons.

The Proper Care of Toys

When new toys first arrive, be sure to discard the plastic wrapping or plastic bags immediately. Check your children's toys often for breakage and potential hazards such as sharp edges or points that may have developed. A damaged or dangerous toy should be thrown away or repaired immediately.

Edges on wooden toys that might have become sharp or surfaces covered with splinters should be sanded smooth. When repainting toys or toy boxes, avoid using leftover paint unless the paint was purchased recently, because some older paints contain more lead than new paint. Examine all outdoor toys regularly for rust or weak parts that could be hazardous.

Teach your child to put his toys safely away after playing to avoid tripping. Never allow toys to be left on or near stairways and see that toys used outdoors are stored after play to avoid rust and damage that can be caused by rain or dew.

Make sure your child's toy chest is safe. Use a toy chest that has a lid that will stay open in any position and will not fall unexpectedly on your child. For extra safety, be sure there are ventilation holes for fresh air. Watch for sharp edges that could cut and hinges that could pinch or squeeze. Refer to Chapter 3 for more safety details about toy boxes.

It is important that you protect your child not only from unsafe toys, but also from the unsafe use of toys. When your child is old enough to understand, teach her to use her toys properly and safely. Careful selection of toys and proper supervision of children at play are still—and always will be— the best way to protect children from toy-related injuries.

On the following pages you will find a comprehensive listing of recommended toys by age group, compiled by the Consumer Product Safety Commission.

Consumer's Guide to Selecting Toys

TOYS FOR YOUNG INFANTS: BIRTH TO 6 MONTHS
ABILITIES AND INTERESTS

PHYSICAL
- visual focus matures—follows objects with eyes
- learns to localize sounds and turns to see
- gains control of hands—learns to bat, then reach and grasp objects
- discovers feet—brings feet to mouth and explores with feet
- begins to sit with support
- large-muscle play may include rolling, scooting, rocking, bouncing

MENTAL
- explores world with eyes and ears and begins to explore with hands and feet and mouth
- enjoys creating effects in the environment by own actions
- begins to recognize familiar people, objects, and events— then to anticipate them
- becomes aware of novelty and strangeness in people, objects, and events
- develops definite preferences for certain people, objects, and events
- may imitate simple movements if in own repertoire
- does one thing at a time

SOCIAL
- special interest in people (faces and voices especially)
- begins to smile at faces, voices, and mirror image
- quiets when there is face and/ or voice contact with people
- begins to seek attention and contact with people
- distinguishes among familiar people and has preferences
- begins to coo and gurgle, babble and laugh aloud, play with sounds
- listens to voices and may imitate sounds already in own repertoire

ALL TOYS	ACTIVE PLAY	MANIPULATIVE PLAY
Toys for this age are primarily for: looking, listening, sucking, or fingering	PUSH AND PULL TOYS *not suited to age group*	CONSTRUCTION TOYS *from about 4 months:* - soft blocks
Infants 0–2 months enjoy seeing and hearing interesting things	RIDE-ON TOYS *not suited to age group*	PUZZLES *not suited to age group*
Infants 2–6 months show growing interest in touching, holding, batting, turning, shaking, kicking, mouthing, and tasting objects	OUTDOOR OR GYM EQUIPMENT *infant swings (with adult supervision)*	PATTERN-MAKING TOYS *not suited to age group* MANIPULATIVE TOYS *from about 6–8 weeks:* - simple rattles - teethers - light, sturdy cloth toys - squeeze toys - toys suspended above or to the side of infant for batting and grasping
Infants like to see: - bright primary colors - high contrast - simple design - clear lines and features - human face features (especially eyes) - bull's-eye pattern		*from about 4 months:* - nipple balls - disks, keys on ring - interlocking plastic rings - small hand-held manipulables - toys on suction cups - crib gyms
Infants enjoy watching hanging objects or "mobiles" that move by wind, wind-up action, or the infant's own activity		
Toys for watching only should be suspended 8–14 inches from the infant's eyes at first and angled toward his eyes, then moved up out of reach when he can touch them		

ALL TOYS

Toys for watching are more appealing if they move and make noise (but movement should be slow and noise not too loud or sudden)

Infants enjoy variety

Infants enjoy producing effects on toys by their own activity

Toys for holding should be light and easily graspable, and mouthable toys should have all safety features recommended for infants:
* no sharp points or edges
* no small parts to be lodged in throat, ears, nose
* no electrical parts
* nontoxic materials
* no glass or brittle plastic
* no parts to entrap fingers, toes, hands

ACTIVE PLAY

SPORTS EQUIPMENT
from about 6–8 weeks:
* clutch balls
* texture balls
* soft squeeze balls

MANIPULATIVE PLAY

DRESSING, LACING, STRINGING TOYS
not suited to age group

SAND AND WATER PLAY TOYS
not suited to age group

MAKE-BELIEVE PLAY

DOLLS
* soft baby dolls, soft-bodied dolls, or rag dolls—all with molded (not loose) hair

STUFFED TOYS
* small plush animals
* music-box animals (operated and monitored for safety by adults)
* grab-on soft toys

PUPPETS
* soft hand puppets (held and moved by adults)

ROLE-PLAY MATERIALS
* mirrors (large, unbreakable) fastened to crib, playpen, or wall (peak interest in mirrors 4–6 months)

PLAY SCENES
not suited to age group

TRANSPORTATION TOYS
not suited to age group

PROJECTILE TOYS
not suited to age group

CREATIVE PLAY
(arts, crafts, music)

MUSICAL INSTRUMENTS
from about 6–8 weeks:
* bell on handle
* wrist bells on ankle
* rattles

ARTS-AND-CRAFTS MATERIALS
not suited to age group

AUDIOVISUAL EQUIPMENT
* phonograph or tape recorder (adult-operated)
* records or tapes (gentle regular rhythms, lullabies)
* music boxes (adult-operated)

LEARNING PLAY

GAMES
not suited to age group

SPECIFIC SKILL-DEVELOPMENT TOYS
not suited to age group

BOOKS
may enjoy being read to

TOYS FOR OLDER INFANTS: 7 TO 12 MONTHS
ABILITIES AND INTERESTS

PHYSICAL
- begins to sit alone
- begins to creep and crawl onto or into things
- begins to pull to a stand, cruise (walk holding furniture), and walk alone (10–16 months)
- interest in moving about and practicing motor skills
- develops "pincer" (thumb-and-finger) grasp and begins to hold objects with one hand while manipulating them with the other
- with objects wants to: bang, insert, poke, twist, squeeze, drop, shake, bite, throw, open/shut, push/pull, empty/fill, drag along
- enjoys bath play—kicking and splashing

MENTAL
- interest in appearing and disappearing (objects and people)—develops "object permanence" (looks for object out of sight at approximately 11 months)
- interest in container/contained relationship—likes to empty cupboards, drawers, and containers of objects
- interest in letting go and dropping objects (will use string to pull back vanished objects)

- interest in exploration and likes many objects to explore
- likes to operate simple mechanisms (open/shut, push/pull) and create effects
- remembers people, objects, games, actions with toys—shows persistence and interest in novelty
- beginning of interest in picture books

SOCIAL
- may fear strangers or react badly to change—plays best with familiar person nearby
- watches and may imitate others
- sensitive to social approval and disapproval
- interest in getting attention and creating social effects
- enjoys simple social games: "peekaboo," "bye-bye"
- babbles and plays with language—may try to imitate sounds
- recognizes own name and may begin to point to named objects or obey simple commands

ALL TOYS

Infants 7–9 months are interested in longer and more extensive exploration of toys. Infants of this age like to:
- bang
- insert
- poke
- twist
- squeeze
- drop
- shake
- bite
- throw
- open and shut
- empty and fill

Infants 10–12 months show beginning interest in object mastery and like many objects to explore. Infants of this age like:
- stacking
- putting in and taking out
- pouring out
- fitting one object into another
- opening and closing
- pressing levers
- turning things (not unscrewing yet)
- pushing balls and cars

Generally, infants in this age range are interested in:
- operating simple mechanisms
- containers and the container/contained relationship
- appearing and disappearing objects

As at earlier ages, infants enjoy producing effects by their own actions

Toys for infants
- nontoxic materials
- no sharp points or edges
- safe for mouthing
- nonbreakable; no glass or brittle plastic
- no small parts to be lodged in throat, ears, nose
- no parts to entrap fingers, toes, hand

ACTIVE PLAY

PUSH AND PULL TOYS
push toys without rods (simple cars, animals on wheels or rollers)

RIDE-ON TOYS
not suited to age group

OUTDOOR OR GYM EQUIPMENT
infant swings (with adult supervision)
soft low climbing platform for crawlers

SPORTS EQUIPMENT
transparent balls
chime balls
flutter balls
action balls

MANIPULATIVE PLAY

CONSTRUCTION TOYS
soft blocks
rubber blocks
rounded wooden bell blocks

PUZZLES
*from about 10 months:
brightly colored, lightweight crib and playpen puzzles (2–3 pieces)*

PATTERN-MAKING TOYS
not suited to age group

MANIPULATIVE TOYS
teethers
light sturdy cloth toys
toys on suction cups
small, hand-held manipulables
nipple balls
disks/keys on rings
plastic pop beads
drop objects on string
squeeze-squeek toys
roly-poly toys
activity boxes and cubes
pop-up boxes (easy operation)
containers with object to empty and fill

MANIPULATIVE PLAY
rubber or plastic pop beads
simple nesting cups
stacking ring cones (few rings and safe stick)
graspable (unbreakable)
mirror toys which can be held and played with
loses interest in crib gyms and toys suspended above when can sit up and move about (crib gyms can create safety hazards when child can get to hands and knees and should be moved out of reach)

DRESSING, LACING, STRINGING TOYS
not suited to age group

SAND AND WATER PLAY TOYS
activity boxes for bath
simple floating toys

MAKE-BELIEVE PLAY

DOLLS
- soft baby dolls, soft-bodied dolls, or rag dolls—all with molded (not loose) hair

STUFFED TOYS
- small plush animals
- music-box animals (operated and monitored for safety by adult)
- grab or soft toys
- big soft toys for hugging and roughhousing

PUPPETS
- soft hand puppets—child may handle but must be moved as puppets by adult

ROLE-PLAY MATERIALS
low wall-mounted mirrors to see self sit, creep, crawl, etc.

PLAY SCENES
not suited to age group

TRANSPORTATION TOYS
simple push cars (one piece)

PROJECTILE TOYS
not suited to age group

CREATIVE PLAY
(arts, crafts, music)

MUSICAL INSTRUMENTS
- bells on handle
- wrist bells to shake
- rattles
- rubber or wooden blocks that rattle or tinkle

ARTS-AND-CRAFTS MATERIALS
from about 12 months:
- large paper
- large crayons for scribbling

AUDIOVISUAL EQUIPMENT
phonograph or tape recorder (adult-operated)
records or tapes (simple songs, lullabies, music with simple rhythms)
music boxes (adult-operated)

LEARNING PLAY

GAMES
not suited to age group

SPECIFIC SKILL-DEVELOPMENT TOYS
not suited to age group

BOOKS
- cloth books
- plastic books
- small cardboard books
Note: Some children enjoy "lap reading" (being read to) from this age onward. When adult-held, paper picture books are appropriate.

TOYS FOR YOUNG TODDLERS: 1-YEAR-OLDS
ABILITIES AND INTERESTS

PHYSICAL
- endless exercise of physical skills
- likes to lug, dump, push, pull, pile, knock down, empty and fill
- likes to climb—can manage small indoor steps
- manipulation is more exploratory than skillful
- active interest in multiple small objects
- by 2 years, can kick, catch a largish ball
- by 2 years, can string large beads, turn knob, use screw motion

MENTAL
- interest in causing effects
- interest in mechanisms and objects that move or can be moved—prefers action toys
- combines objects with other objects—makes simple block structures, uses simple stacking toys, does simple puzzles
- very curious—constant experimentation with objects

- interest in hidden-object toys
- at 1½ to 2 years, groups/matches similar objects—enjoys simple sorting toys
- identifies objects by pointing—can identify pictures in book
- enjoys water, sand play
- makes marks on paper, scribbles spontaneously
- first imitative play—imitation of adult tasks, especially caretaking and housekeeping tasks

SOCIAL
- mostly solitary play—relates to adults better than to children
- tries to do adult tasks
- expresses affection for others—shows preference for certain soft toys, dolls
- likes being read to, looking at picture books, likes nursery rhymes
- by 1½, enjoys interactive games such as tag

ALL TOYS

Children prefer action toys, toys that produce movement or sounds by child's own efforts
- toys need not be highly detailed but should be realistic looking
- toys should be lightweight for easy lifting, carrying
- bright colors preferred

In play, child is always on the move—large-muscle activities such as running, climbing dominate over small-muscle activies such as exploring objects, constructing

Child beginning to combine, put together objects

Beginning of imitative play

ACTIVE PLAY

PUSH AND PULL TOYS
- push toys with rods (rods with large handles on ends)
- toys to push on floor—simple, sturdy, with large wheels
- special noise and action effects
- for steady walkers, pull toys on strings (broad-based to tip less easily)
from about 1½:
- simple doll carriages and wagons—low, open, big enough for child to get in
- small rocking horses—confined rocking arc, stout handles rather than reins, knee height on child
- push/pull toys filled with multiple objects

RIDE-ON TOYS
- ride-ons propelled by pushing with feet—no pedals, no steering mechanism
- stable ride-ons—4 or more wheels, wheels spaced wide apart, child's feet flat on floor when seated
- ride-ons with storage bins
- ride-ons that make noise, look like animals

MANIPULATIVE PLAY

CONSTRUCTION TOYS
- small lightweight blocks (15–25 pieces)
before 1½, most interlocking mechanisms are too difficult
from around 1½:
- solid wooden unit blocks (20–40)
- large hollow building blocks
- large plastic bricks (2–4 inches) to press together

PUZZLES
- simple pre-puzzles or form board—2–3 pieces, each piece a familiar shape

from around 1½:
puzzles with 3–5 pieces and knobs easier to use (knobs firmly attached)

PATTERN-MAKING TOYS
pegboard with a few large pegs

MANIPULATIVE TOYS
- activity boxes attached to crib or playpen or free-standing—simple action mechanisms (doors, lids, switches)
- hidden-object toys
- simple pop-up toys operated by pushing a button or knob
- nesting cups—round shape, few pieces
- simple stacking toys—few pieces, no order necessary
- shape sorters—a few common shapes

ALL TOYS

Toys should meet safety regulations for age:
- sturdy, unbreakable; not likely to break into small pieces and strong enough for child to stand on or in
- nontoxic materials
- no sharp points or edges
- too large to be lodged in windpipe, ears, nostrils
- no detachable small parts
- no parts that could pinch or entrap fingers, toes, hair
- not put together with easily exposed straight pins, sharp wires, nails
- no electrical parts, unless supervised by adult

ACTIVE PLAY

OUTDOOR AND GYM EQUIPMENT
- all gym equipment needs adult supervision
- low, soft climbing platforms
- tunnels for crawling
- swings (pushed by adult)—seats curved or body-shaped, of energy-absorbing material

from about 1½:
- simple, low climbing structures
- low slides with handrails
- outdoor play equipment with stationary rather than moving parts

SPORTS EQUIPMENT
- soft lightweight balls, especially with interesting visual effects, noises, unpredictable movement
- chime ball, flutter ball
- largish balls (easier for child to maneuver)
- *from around 1½*, interest in small rubber balls (at least 1¼ inches in diameter)

MANIPULATIVE PLAY

from around 1½:
- fit-together toys of about 5 pieces
- activity boxes with more complex action mechanisms—turning knob or dial, turning simple key
- pounding/hammering toys
- nesting toys—square or other shapes
- stacking toys of 4–5 pieces
- simple matching toys
- simple number/counting boards (1–5) with large pegs
- simple lock boxes and lock/key toys
- jack-in-the-box toys (adult supervision if toys spring back quickly)
- toys with screwing action (child can usually manage only 1 turn)

DRESSING, LACING, STRINGING TOYS
- large colored beads (fewer than 10)
from around 1½:
- lacing cubes or board with thick, blunt spindle

SAND AND WATER PLAY TOYS
- simple floating toys—1 or 2 pieces, easy to grasp in one hand
- sponges; small shovel and pail
from around 1½:
- nesting tub toys
- bathtub activity centers
- funnels, colanders
- small sandbox tools (rake should have blunt teeth)

MAKE-BELIEVE PLAY

DOLLS
- soft-bodied or all-rubber baby dolls
- simple dolls—no hair, moving eyes, or movable limbs
- dolls to fit easily in child's arms, or small dolls (5–6 inches)
- simple accessories for care-taking—bottle, blanket
- simple doll clothes, need not be detachable

from around 1½:
- small peg people

STUFFED TOYS
- very soft, lightweight, easy to hold
- slender limbs on toys for easy grasp
- no whiskers, buttons, bows, bells for safety reasons

PUPPETS
- puppets operated by adult

from around 1½:
- small hand puppets sized to fit child's hand
- soft, plush puppets that double as stuffed toys

ROLE-PLAY MATERIALS
- toy telephone; full-length unbreakable mirror (attached to wall)
- simple housekeeping equipment
- simple doll equipment—carriage, bed

from around 1½:
- simple dress-ups—hats, scarves, ties, shoes, jewelry—and role-play toys that can be pushed and make noise—mower, vacuum

CREATIVE PLAY
(arts, crafts, music)

MUSICAL INSTRUMENTS
- rhythm instruments operated by shaking—bells, rattles

from around 1½:
- rhythm instruments operated by banging together—cymbals, drums

ARTS-AND-CRAFTS MATERIALS
- large crayons
- sturdy, large-size paper

AUDIOVISUAL EQUIPMENT
operated by adult:
- tapes and records of nursery rhymes and rhythms
- hand-cranked music box, worked by child if crank is large and easy to turn

LEARNING PLAY

GAMES
not suited to age group

SPECIFIC SKILL-DEVELOPMENT TOYS
not suited to age group

BOOKS
- sturdy cloth, plastic, cardboard books with few pages
- picture books, nursery rhymes, stories with repetition
- books to be held and read by adult can be more fragile, with paper pages

from around 1½:
- touch-me or tactile books

MAKE-BELIEVE PLAY

- child-sized equipment—
  oven, fridge, sink, table
  and chairs

PLAY SCENES
before 1½:
- child may enjoy handling,
  carrying around figures
from around 1½:
- familiar, realistic scenes—
  farms, airport, garage, not
  overly detailed or with lots
  of pieces (4–6 pieces)
- prefer scenes with mov-
  ing parts or that make
  noise

TRANSPORTATION TOYS
- lightweight vehicles of a
  size for easy handling
  (not too small)
- push or pull cars and
  trains
- vehicles that make noise
- first train—1–2 cars, no
  tracks, simple or no coupling system
from around 1½:
- more detailed vehicles—
  doors, hoods that open
- trains with simple cou-
  pling system—large
  hooks, magnets

PROJECTILE TOYS
not suited to age group

TOYS FOR OLDER TODDLERS: 2-YEAR-OLDS
ABILITIES AND INTERESTS

PHYSICAL
- skilled at most simple large-muscle skills
- lots of physical testing—jumping from heights, climbing, hanging by arms, rolling, galloping, somersaults, rough-and-tumble play
- throws and retrieves all kinds of objects
- pushes self on wheeled objects with good steering
- by 2½ to 3 years, good hand and finger coordination
- lots of active play with small objects—explores different qualities of play materials

MENTAL
- interested in attributes of objects—texture, shape, size, color
- can match a group of similar objects
- plays with pattern, sequence, order of size
- first counting skills

- first creative activities (drawing, construction, clay)—process still more important than final product
- beginning to solve problems in head
- imaginative fantasy play increases—continued interest in domestic imitation
- fantasy play alone or with adult—child also makes toys carry out actions on other toys

SOCIAL
- main interest still in parents, but begins to play cooperatively with other children (especially 2½ to 3 years)
- uses language to express wishes to others
- engages in game-like interactions with others—also some pretend play with others
- enjoys hearing simple stories read from picture books, especially stories with repetition
- strong desire for independence—shows pride in accomplishment

ALL TOYS

Beginning of cooperative, social play

Increasing interest in pretend play

Love of physical, active play

Child prefers action toys, toys that produce movement or sounds by child's own efforts

More realism preferred
* beginning to pay attention to qualities of objects
* prefers toys with working parts

Toys should be lightweight enough for easy lifting, carrying

Bright colors preferred

ACTIVE PLAY

PUSH AND PULL TOYS
* pull toys with strings
* doll carriages
* wagons
* small, light wheelbarrow
* interest in push toys that look like adult equipment—lawn mower, vacuum, shopping cart

RIDE-ON TOYS
*. interest in realistic-looking ride-ons—tractors, motorcycles
* ride-ons with storage trays or bins
* ride-ons propelled by bouncing up and down
* when children begin to pedal (around 2½–3), small tricycle (wheels 10–13 inches)

OUTDOOR AND GYM EQUIPMENT
* all gym equipment needs adult supervision
* tunnels
* climbing structures and slides
* stationary rather than moving outdoor equipment
* swings with curved, soft seats

MANIPULATIVE PLAY

CONSTRUCTION TOYS
* solid, wooden unit blocks
* large, hollow building blocks (cardboard, wood, plastic)
* large, plastic bricks (2–4 inches) to be pressed together
* plastic interlocking rings; large plastic nuts and bolts

PUZZLES
* fit-in puzzles
* 2 to 2½ years, 4–5 pieces
* 2½ to 3 years, 6–12 pieces
* puzzles with knobs easier (knobs should be firmly attached)

PATTERN-MAKING TOYS
* pegboards with large pegs
* color cubes
* magnetic boards with shapes, animals, people
* color forms (from around 2½)

MANIPULATIVE TOYS
* fit-together toys of 5–10 pieces
* nesting toys with multiple pieces, including barrel toys that require screwing motion

ALL TOYS

Toys should meet safety regulations for age:
- sturdy, unbreakable; not likely to break into small pieces and strong enough for child to stand on or in
- nontoxic materials
- no sharp points or edges
- too large to be lodged in windpipe, ears, nostrils
- no detachable small parts
- no parts that could pinch or entrap fingers, toes, hair
- not put together with easily exposed straight pins, sharp wires, nails
- no electrical parts, unless supervised by adult

ACTIVE PLAY

SPORTS EQUIPMENT
- balls of all sizes, but especially large balls
- sleds sized to child (shorter length than child's height)
- ball darts
- spinning seat
- pool toys (tubes, mats) with adult supervision

MANIPULATIVE PLAY
- number/counting boards with large pegs
- shape sorters with common shapes
- pounding/hammering toys
- smelling jars
- feel bag or box
- color/picture dominoes
- simple lotto matching games based on color, pictures

DRESSING, LACING, STRINGING TOYS
- large, colored beads
- lacing card or wooden shoe for lacing
- dressing books and dolls
- frames, cubes for lacing, buttoning, snapping, hooking

SAND AND WATER PLAY TOYS
- bathtub activity centers
- nesting tub toys
- tub toys with removable figures, accessories
- linking tub toys
- small boats (no metal parts)
- small and large sandbox tools (with blunt edges)
- water/sand mills
- sprinklers

MAKE-BELIEVE PLAY

DOLLS
- soft-bodied and rubber baby dolls
- more realistic dolls with hair and moving eyes
- dolls to fit in child's arms; also small, realistic dolls
- talking dolls operated by pulling string
- small peg dolls
- doll accessories—simple and sturdy
- caretaking accessories—bottle, blanket
- simple removable garments (hook and loop, large snap fasteners)

STUFFED TOYS
- soft, pliable animals
- mother and baby combinations
- preference for realistic animals, replicas of familiar characters

CREATIVE PLAY
(arts, crafts, music)

MUSICAL INSTRUMENTS
- all rhythm instruments—bells, rattles, cymbals, drums, triangle, rhythm stick, sand blocks
- horns and whistles (around 2½)

ARTS-AND-CRAFTS MATERIALS
- large crayons
- paints (finger and tempera) and brushes with blunt ends
- clay
- sturdy markers
- blunt-end scissors
- chalkboard, large chalk
- colored construction paper

AUDIOVISUAL EQUIPMENT
- operated by adult: tapes, records
- hand-cranked music box if crank is large and easy to turn

LEARNING PLAY

GAMES
- lotto matching games based on color pictures
- dominoes, especially giant dominoes
- board games based on chance—only a few pieces or pairs

SPECIFIC SKILL-DEVELOPMENT TOYS
simple teaching toys for:
- matching/sorting, shapes, colors, letters/sounds, numbers, concepts
- all electrically powered toys need adult supervision

BOOKS
- sturdy books with heavy paper, cardboard pages
- short simple stories with repetition and familiar subjects

MAKE-BELIEVE PLAY	CREATIVE PLAY (arts, crafts, music)	LEARNING PLAY

MAKE-BELIEVE PLAY

- toys with music box inside

PUPPETS
- small hand puppets (hand-and-arm puppets too large)
- lightweight, sized to fit child's hand
- puppets doubling as stuffed toys
- puppets representing familiar characters

ROLE-PLAY MATERIALS
- dress-ups and costumes
- equipment should be realistic-looking
- child-sized equipment—stove, cooking board, refrigerator
- doll equipment
- all housekeeping equipment—cleaning sets, pots and pans, bath and laundry
- toys that can be pushed—vacuum, lawn-mower, shopping cart
- full-length, unbreakable mirror

PLAY SCENES
- familiar, realistic-looking scenes—farms, garage, airport
- scenes with multiple pieces but not highly detailed
- preference for moving parts, parts that make noise
- interior of scenes easily accessible
- vehicle sets with figures

TRANSPORTATION TOYS
- small, realistic cars (not metal)
- vehicles with moving parts
- large trucks (metal too heavy)—moving parts, parts operated by large lever (with knob on end)
- cars, trucks with removable figures, accessories
- small trains with simple coupling mechanism—no tracks

PROJECTILE TOYS
not suited to age group

LEARNING PLAY

- simple pictures with clear color, few details
- pop-up books
- hidden picture books
- dressing books

TOYS FOR PRESCHOOLERS:
3, 4, AND 5 YEARS
ABILITIES AND INTERESTS

PHYSICAL
- runs, jumps, climbs, balances with assurance—by 5, gross motor skills are well developed
- likes risks, tests of physical strength and skill—loves acrobatics and outdoor equipment
- increasing finger control—can pick up small objects, cut on a line with scissors, hold pencil in adult grasp, string small beads
- expert builder—loves small constuction materials and also vigorous activity with big blocks, large construction materials
- by 5, rudimentary interest in ball games with simple rules and scoring

MENTAL
- familiar with common shapes, primary colors
- interest in simple number activities, alphabet play, copying letters, matching/sorting
- by 5, sorts and matches using more than one quality at a time
- around 4, begins to be purposeful and goal-directed, to make use of a plan

- interest in producing designs, including puzzles, and in constructing play worlds
- first representational pictures
- prefers realism
- interest in nature, science, animals, time, how things work
- peak interest in dramatic play—re-creates adult occupations, uses costumes and props

SOCIAL
- beginning to share and take turns; learning concept of fair play
- by 5, play is cooperative, practical, conforming
- interested in group pretend play
- not ready for competitive play because hates to lose
- enjoys simple board games based on chance, not strategy
- more sex differentiation in play roles, interests
- enjoys looking at books and being read to

ALL TOYS

Preschoolers prefer toys with realistic detail and working parts

Increasing interest in dramatic and pretend play; *by age 5*, peak period for dramatic play, with all sorts of props

Period of peak interest in puppet play

Increasing construction activity, often with plan or goal

Period of peak interest in play scenes, small figures and cars

ACTIVE PLAY

PUSH AND PULL TOYS
- small wagons
- small wheelbarrow
- push toys resembling adult tools—lawn mowers, vacuum, shopping cart
- doll carriages and strollers
from age 5:
- full-size wagons, scooters

RIDE-ON TOYS
- tricycles sized to child
- 3- and 4-wheel pedal toys
- vehicles with steering mechanisms
- prefers realistic, detailed vehicles
- full-size rocking horse
from age 4:
- low-slung tricycles
- battery-operated ride-ons
from age 5:
- small bicycle with training wheels and foot brakes, sized to child

OUTDOOR AND GYM EQUIPMENT
- adult supervision recommended for gym equipment
- stationary outdoor climbing equipment
- slides (with side rails) and ladders
- swings with curved, soft seats
- balance board

MANIPULATIVE PLAY

CONSTRUCTION TOYS
- solid wooden unit blocks—large and small
- large hollow blocks
- plastic blocks to be pressed together (2–4 inches)
from age 4:
- most types of interlocking building systems, pieces of all sizes (plastic rather than metal pieces)
- no motorized parts
from age 5:
- prefers sets that make realistic models
- can connect pieces in specific order to create simple models

PUZZLES
- fit-in or framed puzzles: *age 3*, up to 20 pieces; *age 4*, 20–30 pieces; *age 5*, up to 50 pieces
- large, simple jigsaw puzzles (10–25 pieces)
- number or letter puzzles; puzzle clocks
- cardboard puzzles

PATTERN-MAKING TOYS
- bead stringing—longer, thinner string (with stiff tip) large beads
- pegboard with small pegs
- color cubes/color forms
- magnetic boards with shapes

ALL TOYS

Toys should be sturdy:
- not likely to break easily into small pieces or leave jagged edges
- no sharp points or edges
- not made of glass or brittle plastic

Toys should be of nontoxic materials

Toys should have no electrical parts unless supervised by adult

ACTIVE PLAY

from age 4:
- equipment with movable parts: small seesaws, hanging rings
- swings with flat seats
- rope ladders and ropes
- gym sets with enclosures for pretend house or fort

SPORTS EQUIPMENT
- balls of all shapes, sizes
- double-blade ice skates
- sleds size-graded (no hand brakes or steering wheels)
from age 4:
- lightweight soft baseball and bat
- junior-sized soccer ball, football
- speed-graded roller skates (plastic wheels, no ball bearings for reduced speed)
- kites
- wading pool
from age 5:
- jump ropes
- skis (sized to child)
- flying disks (especially lightweight ones)
- magnetic darts
- inner tubes, kickboards, mattresses for beginning swimmers (adult supervision needed)

MANIPULATIVE PLAY

from age 4:
beginning interest in design materials—mosaic blocks, felt boards; can follow, copy simple sequence
from age 5:
simple weaving (looper and heddle loom) small beads to string (½ inch); block printing equipment

MANIPULATIVE TOYS
- matching toys by color, shape, or picture; *from age 4*, by concept, letters (ABC), numbers (1–10)
- sorting toys; number rods
- number boards with small pegs
- simple counting toys; lock boxes
- nesting toys with multiple pieces and screw closing
from age 4:
geometrical concept toys
from age 5:
simple models of mechanical devices or natural objects; more complex lotto matching toys

DRESSING, LACING, STRINGING TOYS
frames/cards to button, hook, tie
from age 5:
simple sewing kits with thick cloth and large blunt needle (with supervision)

SAND AND WATER PLAY TOYS
- large and small sandbox tools; bubbles
- wind-up bath toys; bath activity centers
from age 4:
- sand molds; water pump
- realistic working models of boats (no sharp metal parts)

MAKE-BELIEVE PLAY

DOLLS
- realistic dolls with detail and accessories, especially baby dolls
- dolls with hair, moving eyes, movable limbs, special features

from age 5:
- child-proportioned dolls (can dress dolls if garments and fastenings are simple)
- paper dolls to be punched out

STUFFED TOYS
- stuffed toys with accessories—ribbons, bells, simple clothes
- realistic-looking toys, replicas of famous characters
- music-box toys

from age 5:
collecting toys in sets

PUPPETS
- simple sock or mitten puppets
- finger puppets
- simple puppet theater (no scenery)

from age 5:
hand-and-arm puppets; more detailed puppets; puppets with limbs

ROLE-PLAY MATERIALS
- dress-ups, costumes of all types
- realistic, detailed equipment—*by 5*, want it to really work
- housekeeping and cooking equipment
- toy telephone; toy camera; doctor kits
- military costumes and props
- specialized doll equipment
- cash register, equipment to play store
- play stages; large unbreakable mirror

PLAY SCENES
- scenes with a variety of realistic accessories and working parts

CREATIVE PLAY
(arts, crafts, music)

MUSICAL INSTRUMENTS
- all rhythm instruments
- xylophones
- instruments that require blowing—harmonica, horns, whistles, simple recorder
- wind-up music boxes
- piano—one-finger tunes

ARTS-AND-CRAFTS MATERIALS
- large crayons with many colors
- color paddles
- magic markers
- finger and tempera paint
- adjustable easel
- brushes of various sizes
- clay, including modeling clay and tools
- chalkboards and chalk of various sizes
- scissors with rounded ends
- paste and glue
- simple block printing equipment
- pop-it beads
- large beads to string
- simple sewing kits (without needles)

from age 4:
- increased interest in art products; also, can copy order
- workbench and hammer, nails, saw

from age 5:
- smaller crayons; coloring books; watercolor paints; simple weaving loom, small beads to string; sewing kits with large blunt needles

AUDIOVISUAL EQUIPMENT
- hand-cranked music boxes
- parent-operated record and tape player

from age 4:
- record and tape players for child to operate
- simple video games

from age 5:
- radio

LEARNING PLAY

- pool toys (tubes, mats) with adult supervision

GAMES
- dominoes (color or number)
- simple matching and lotto games based on color, pictures
- simple card games
- bingo (picture)

from age 4:
- first board games, based completely on chance— games should have few rules, simple scoring, no reading required beyond ABC, only a few pieces
- games requiring simple fine-motor coordination (picking up or balancing objects)

SPECIFIC SKILLS-DEVELOPMENT TOYS
simple electronic and other teaching toys for:
- matching/sorting
- shapes, colors
- numbers and letters

from age 4:
- simple computer programs for teaching color matching, letters, classification, numbers, sounds
- simple science models

from age 5:
- science materials—magnets, flashlight, shells and rocks, magnifying glass, stethoscope, prism, aquarium, terrarium
- clock
- printing set
- toy typewriter
- simple calculator
- computer programs to teach simple programming

BOOKS
- picture books, simple stories, rhymes
- complex pop-up books
- likes complex illustrations with an abundance of detail

age 3 interests:
- here-and-now stories

MAKE-BELIEVE PLAY

- favorite themes—garage, farm, airport, space, forts
- action/adventure sets; action figures
- first doll house—simple, few rooms; easy access, space to move objects around, sturdy furnishings

from age 5:
- can manipulate very small pieces; attention to realistic detail

TRANSPORTATION TOYS

- toy cars of all sizes— small metal cars, trucks with very realistic detail
- large-scale trucks, road machinery that really works (dumps, digs)
- action/adventure vehicle sets
- small, realistic trains

from age 5:
small trains with tracks: can work most train coupling systems; can plan, build simple track layouts; wind-up and spring-driven cars

PROJECTILE TOYS—*none before age 4*

- soft, flexible projectiles
- action figures with projectile weapons

from age 5:
- guns shooting ping-pong balls, soft darts, helicopter-type projectiles

CREATIVE PLAY
(arts, crafts, music)

LEARNING PLAY

- animal stories
- alphabet books
- words and rhymes

age 4 interests:
- wild stories, silly humor
- information books
- familiar places, people

age 5 interests:
- realistic stories
- poetry
- primers
- animals who behave like people

Babysitters

Watching children is an important job

SELECTING A COMPE-
tent babysitter is an extremely important job. When you
leave the house you are placing that person in a position of
full responsibility for the safety of your home and your child.

Too often, this selection process is done on a last-minute basis when the only criterion is availability.

When you are selecting a babysitter, check references carefully. You'll want to make sure the person is capable of maintaining safety and protection, has a sense of responsibility, and is old enough and capable enough to assume that responsibility.

Once you have selected a babysitter, plan part of a day or evening to spend some time with her before an actual "sitting" job. It may be a good idea to make sure your sitter is educated on safety by loaning the sitter this book to read.

Make sure you cover the following points in your initial meeting:

- Have the sitter become acquainted with your children and their routine.
- Show the sitter around the house, pointing out the fire escape routes and the location of fire extinguishers and indicating any potential problem areas.
- Show the sitter where your emergency phone list is kept as well as the number where you can be reached and the number of a nearby relative or neighbor who will be in while you're gone.
- Show the sitter where the flashlight and first-aid kit are kept and how your baby equipment and safety devices work.
- Discuss the feeding, bathing, and sleeping arrangements for your children. Include a list of what your children are allowed to eat and drink and when, what time naps and bedtime are scheduled, what activities your children enjoy, and what things are not allowed.
- Tell the sitter of any allergies or specific medical needs of your children and show where the medicine is kept and how to administer it.

Instruct your sitter to:

- Never leave the children alone in the house, even for a moment.
- Keep the doors locked at all times.
- Always phone for help if concerned or in doubt.
- Never allow friends in your home unless this has been agreed upon with you in advance, and *never* open the door to a stranger.
- Never tell a phone caller you are alone—just say we are unavailable and take a message.
- Stay alert and not be distracted by personal phone calls or a blaring radio, stereo, or television.
- Never give any medicine or food to your children unless instructed to do so.
- Never take the children away from the house unless this has been agreed upon with you in advance or an emergency requires evacuation of the house.
- In the case of smoke or fire, get the children out immediately without stopping to dress them or make a phone call. Take the children to a neighbor, then call the fire department first and you second.

Watching children is an important job, so it's best not to expect much more than this from your sitter. For instance, it may not be a good idea to have a babysitter bathe your infant or small toddler. If meal preparation is required, try to keep it simple and cleanup to a minimum. If there is some "picking up" required, the sitter should save this until after the children are asleep. Just make sure the sitter understands that the primary job is to watch your children.

9

Fire Safety

The it-can't-possibly-happen-here attitude is very common when it comes to fire safety

THE MOST UNUSUAL thing about fire safety, if you ask most people, is that a fire is something that always happens to somebody else. It's something you watch at the end of the late news, something that everyone views with a curious sense of detachment.

After all, it was a run-down property, or perhaps they had been careless? The it-can't-possibly-happen-here attitude is very common when it comes to fire safety.

If you doubt this, just put this book down for a minute and go count your fire extinguishers. If you have even one, you're doing better than most. In any case, let's review your home from the standpoint of fire safety. The possibility of a fire, no matter how remote, should not be considered lightly. The implications are just too serious for you and your family.

All about Fire Extinguishers

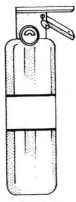

It's important that you have a fire extinguisher for any area of your home where there is a fire risk. Kitchen, workshop, basement, and garage are the most common high-risk areas.

Fire extinguishers contain certain chemicals for different kinds of fires:

A typical fire extinguisher

- Type A extinguishers are for putting out burning wood, paper, cloth, rubber, and plastics.
- Type B extinguishers are for flammable liquids such as gasoline, paint, solvents, kitchen grease, and oil.
- Type C extinguishers are for electrical fires.
- Type A-B-C extinguishers contain multipurpose chemicals that can put out almost all fires.

The best choice is to have Type A-B-C extinguishers and to make sure they are UL approved. Have your extinguishers inspected and recharged about once a year. If you use the extinguisher, have it recharged immediately, even if you have only partially used it. Many fire departments offer free inspection and recharging for home units. If your fire department does not, check your phone book under "Fire Extinguishers" for a company that offers this service.

Make sure that you and all responsible family members and babysitters know where the extinguishers are kept and how to use them. Read the manufacturer's instructions and contact your fire department if you have any questions. As a general rule, the best way to use a fire extinguisher is to aim it at the base of the fire and sweep it back and forth. Always keep your back to an exit so that you can escape quickly if the extinguisher does not put out the fire.

It's very important to remember that a fire extinguisher is for a *small* fire. Get your family outside to safety and call the fire department from a neighbor's phone for a larger fire—the fire department has the equipment and training to fight larger fires.

Fire-Prevention Tips

In addition to a few well-placed fire extinguishers, there are safety tips to keep in mind.

KITCHEN FIRE-PREVENTION TIPS

- Stay in the kitchen whenever cooking something on top of the stove. When frying, keep the pan's lid handy.
- Don't hang spice racks, pot holders, or dish towels over stoves because they can catch fire. For the same reason, you should not wear loose-fitting sleeves while cooking.
- Keep broilers, ovens, and ventilation ducts and hoods clean and free of grease.
- To extinguish a grease fire, cover the pan with a lid

and turn the burner off. Lack of oxygen will put out the fire. Never throw water on a grease fire—it will spread the flames and splatter the hot grease.

- To extinguish a fire in the oven or broiler, close the oven or broiler door and turn off the heat.

FIRE-PREVENTION TIPS FOR FIREPLACES AND WOOD STOVES

- Never leave your child alone in a room where a fire is burning in a fireplace or wood stove. An unlit fireplace can be dangerous, too. Make sure it has a sturdy metal screen or tempered glass doors to keep your child away from the ashes and soot. Lock away heavy or sharp fireplace tools when they're not in use.
- Wood stoves should be made of cast iron or heavy steel and have a damper for draft control. There should be a clearance of at least 36 inches between the stove and combustible walls or ceilings. The stove should be on a base of noncombustible material such as metal or brick which extends at least 18 inches beyond the stove in all directions.
- Once a year you should have your chimney professionally cleaned and checked for crumbling bricks, loose mortar, obstructions, and creosote buildup. A dirty chimney on a fireplace or wood stove can cause a chimney fire. Also, make sure your chimney cap has a spark arrestor to keep burning ashes and sparks from leaping out of the chimney to the roof or yard.
- Make sure the fire is out in your fireplace or wood stove before you go to bed.
- Never start a fire in a fireplace or wood stove with charcoal starter or gasoline.
- Leave the door on a wood stove closed at all times.
- Burn only dry, well-seasoned hardwoods such as

maple, elm, birch, and oak. Avoid pine, spruce, and wood that is green and moist. Some very dangerous materials in a fireplace or stove are colored newspapers, gift wrap, and magazines (some contain chemicals or inks that create unhealthy fumes), aerosol cans (can explode), and dry evergreen branches (can cause an inferno).

- Keep draperies and furniture or anything combustible at least three feet from a wood stove or fireplace.
- Don't dispose of fireplace or stove ashes until they are cold. Carry and dispose of them in a metal container as an added precaution.
- Don't use cooking grills in the fireplace. Meat drippings and oil can ignite and cause flames to leap out of the fireplace.
- Your fireplace should have a screen that covers the entire opening to keep sparks from flying out of the fireplace.

FIRE-PREVENTION TIPS FOR FURNACES AND HEATERS

- If you have a furnace, you should have a qualified service person clean and check your unit and controls at least once a year. He will make sure the emergency shutoff is working and see that the flue pipes are clean, well supported, and free of holes. Make sure you change or clean the furnace filter regularly to avoid overtaxing the furnace.
- Make sure to keep anything combustible—such as papers, paint, rags, etc.—away from the furnace.
- If you use a portable electric space heater, make sure it has a safety switch that automatically shuts it off if it is tipped over. (If your heater has the "UL-approved" mark, it has such a safety switch.)

- Don't use kerosene heaters indoors. They cause indoor air pollution and they are especially dangerous if children are present. It's improtant to note that the exhaust from a vacuum cleaner can spread the flames of a kerosene heater onto carpets and drapes or other materials in a room. If you insist on using a kerosene heater, use only K-1, water-clear kerosene. When you add fuel, take the heater or the tank outdoors. Never fill or move the heater while it is still hot. Never leave your child alone in a room with the heater. Make sure the room has a window open at least one inch for ventilation and never use a kerosene heater while sleeping or away from the house.
- If you have baseboard heaters, make sure that nothing is touching them—furniture, draperies, blankets, electrical cords, etc. The heat from a baseboard heater can become hot enough to ignite or melt things that are in prolonged contact with it.
- Don't use extension cords with portable heaters unless they are designed for the heavier power load, and never use an electric heater in a damp or wet area.

OTHER FIRE-PREVENTION TIPS

- Discard trash promptly, especially if it contains oily or paint-saturated rags or other combustible items.
- Don't store gasoline in the house. Discard old paint thinners and solvents at an authorized chemical disposal company. Oily clothes must be rinsed and then discarded. Keep combustible liquids in a tightly closed metal container and store them in a cool place.
- Never use pennies or other substitutes for fuses and never use a fuse of a higher amperage than the one specified.
- Overloaded electrical systems can cause fire. Watch for

overload signals: dimming lights when an appliance goes on; slow-heating appliances; fuses blowing frequently. Periodically check all electrical and appliance cords—look for frayed insulation, loose connections, damaged cords, faulty switches, and loose wall receptacles.

- Never overload electrical outlets by using extenders, and make sure extension cords match the wattage of the appliance they are being used with.
- Never allow anyone to smoke in a chair, sofa, or bed when drowsy. Use large, deep ashtrays and empty them regularly. Keep matches and lighters where children can't reach them.

Smoke Detectors

The most important thing you can do for your family's fire safety is to properly install and maintain home smoke detectors. Smoke detectors can sense the rising smoke from a fire and sound an alarm loud enough to be heard throughout your house and to awaken those who are sleeping. Even if you already have smoke detectors in your home, read this section carefully. There may be some important information here that you're not aware of.

There are two types of smoke detectors:

1. *Ionization-chamber detectors* use a radioactive source to produce electrically charged molecules (ions) in the air. This sets up an electric current within the detector's chamber so that when smoke enters the chamber, it attaches itself to the ions and reduces the flow of electric current, which sets off the alarm. This type of detector responds faster to flaming fires.
2. *Photoelectric detectors* activate when smoke is dense enough to deflect its beam of light. This type of de-

tector reacts more quickly to smoldering fires, even if there are no flames.

Because most home fires produce a mixture of smoke types, either an ionization or a photoelectric detector will meet most home needs.

SELECTION AND LOCATION OF SMOKE DETECTORS

You should install at least one smoke detector on every floor of your home. Even though an upstairs detector will sense smoke no matter where it originates, a downstairs detector will react sooner to a fire which could block escape routes through the first floor. For instance, locating a detector on the basement ceiling near the steps to the rest of the house is advisable.

There are two big advantages to having two or more units. You will be able to have both an ionization and a photoelectric model, giving you the best capabilities of both. You will be able to equip your home with at least one battery-powered unit and one plug-in or wired-in model so that neither battery failure nor power outage can leave your family unprotected.

When purchasing new smoke detectors, look for a laboratory seal of approval or a statement on the package or unit itself that the detector has been tested and certified by a recognized testing organization. This seal ensures that the unit meets certain standards of operation and sensitivity. Make sure that clear and detailed installation and maintenance instructions accompany the unit. The instructions should tell you how to install it, suggest where to put it, and provide guidelines for testing and maintenance.

Since the primary job of a smoke detector is to wake up sleepers, you should locate your smoke detectors as close as possible to the bedrooms. If sleeping areas are separated, each should have its own detector. The hallway adjacent to the bedrooms is a priority location for a smoke detector. If you have a single-level home, a detector should be placed in the hallway near the bedrooms. If your home has the bedrooms upstairs, a detector should be placed near the top of the stairs leading to the bedrooms. If a bedroom door is normally kept closed at night, you should consider locating a detector inside that room as well—especially if the occupant smokes in bed or if it is your child's room.

There are some places *not* to put a smoke detector. Make sure not to locate a detector within six inches of where a wall and ceiling meet or anywhere near a fan or heating and cooling ducts. Smoke detectors placed in these locations may not receive the flow of smoke required to activate the detector. Ionization detectors can react to extreme changes in humidity, so it's best not to use them near kitchens, bathrooms, water heaters, etc. In these areas you should use a photoelectric detector.

TESTING AND MAINTENANCE OF SMOKE DETECTORS

Your smoke detectors should be tested at least once a month. Check the testing instructions on your smoke detectors. Some of the newer units have more functional testing systems which simulate the presence of smoke, but on many of the older units the "test" button only activates the warning horn and does not tell you whether the detector circuit itself is working. For a unit that does not have a functional testing system, test it by holding a lit candle about six inches below it. If it is an ionization detector, let the flame burn. If it is a photoelectric detector, blow out the candle and let the candle's smoke drift into the detector. Within about 20 seconds, the alarm should begin to sound.

To stop the alarm, fan the smoke away from the unit and the detector will soon stop sounding.

Keep your smoke detectors clean by following the manufacturer's instructions for cleaning. Batteries should be replaced at least once a year. Or when your battery-powered detector emits its low-power warning, remove the weak battery and replace it immediately with a new one. Keep new batteries on hand at all times. If you have a photoelectric detector, you should also keep replacement lamps (the lights that create the beam) on hand.

FALSE ALARMS

Never respond to false alarms caused by cooking, fireplaces, etc., by disconnecting the battery or unplugging the unit. You should either fan away the smoke, relocate the detector, or puchase a detector with a delay switch for that location. A delay switch is useful in a room like the kitchen because it requires a certain amount of time before the alarm responds to the smoke.

Remind everyone in your family that the smoke detectors are not toys and should not be operated, or even touched, except for testing and maintenance.

Your Family's Fire Escape Plan

Every family member needs to know what to do in case of a fire. Design a fire escape plan for your home and practice it with your family so that if the smoke detector sounds, everyone will know exactly what to do.

Here are some important rules about escaping a fire:

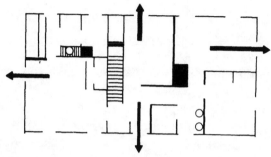

Develop your own fire escape plan

- Your escape plan should include a main and alternate exit from each room, especially bedrooms.
- If your second way out of a two-story home is a window, invest in a portable escape ladder, keep it handy, and make sure all family members and babysitters know where it is located and how to use it.

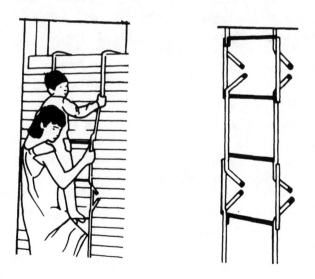

Stabilizing bars make for a safer descent (with bars marked)

- If you live in an apartment building, know and practice with your family two ways out of the building. Leave elevators out of your escape plan because they can become trapped between floors or take you to the fire floor.
- Part of your plan should include a safe meeting place outside the building where every member of the household is to gather so you will know that the entire family has escaped safely.
- The most important part of home escape is getting out safely. Emphasize that everyone should go outside first and then call the fire department from a neighboring home. It's especially important to teach children never to go back into the house after they escape, and never to hide under beds or in closets.
- During an escape, test doors before opening them. If the knob or door is hot, use an alternate exit. If you are on the first floor, you can climb out a window. On higher floors, if there is a balcony or roof outside your window, wait there if an escape ladder is not available.
- When your escape route is smoky, crawl low, keeping your head down, away from the smoke. This is the way firefighters enter a burning building because the cleaner air is nearer to the floor or ground.
- If smoke, heat, or fire blocks an escape, stay in the room and close the door. If the room has a phone, call the emergency number. While you are waiting for help, seal off the cracks around the door with sheets, blankets, or clothing. If smoke and fire aren't rising from below, open the windows for air and hang a sheet or a piece of clothing out to signal for help. Until help arrives, stay low to the floor where the air will be cooler and less smoky. If water is available, wet a towel or piece of clothing and hold it to your face to help filter the smoke.
- Teach all family members the rule of "Stop, Drop, and

Roll." If clothing catches fire, don't run—running will only make the fire burn more. *STOP* where you are, *DROP* to the floor or ground, and *ROLL* or rock over the burning clothing to put out the flames. You can also wrap yourself in a blanket or rug to put a fire out.

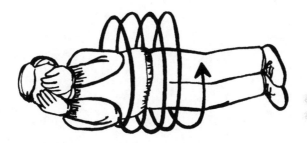

Teach all family members the rule of "Stop, Drop, and Roll"

Practice drills are an important part of your plan. Involve every member of your household in them—your children and the babysitters, too. Practice the escape at night, which is when most dangerous fires occur. You may want to consider taking your children to a neighboring firehouse to see the equipment and protective gear the firefighters use. That way, they won't be frightened of firefighters if they are being rescued in a fire. And be sure to keep your fire department's phone number on or near every phone in your home.

It's important for you to know that few people burn to death in fires. Most people die from the smoke and poisonous gases because they don't know what to do or don't act quickly enough. So if you have an escape plan and use it during an emergency, you will greatly increase your family's safety.

10

First Aid

It's important for you to be prepared for anything from
a tiny scratch to a serious bump on the head

ACCIDENTS CAN OCCUR
even in the most conscientious families, so it is important
for you to be prepared for anything from a tiny scratch or
splinter to a serious bump on the head.

These are the steps you can take to be prepared:

- Keep a well-stocked first-aid kit.
- Take a course in first aid and CPR and/or invest in a good first-aid reference book (see Appendix D).
- Know who and how to call for help.

Your First-Aid Kit

A well-stocked first-aid kit is a necessity for your home

Minor scratches, cuts, bruises, and bumps are the most common injuries your young child is likely to encounter. A well-stocked first-aid kit will generally get you through these minor emergencies and help bring a smile back to the face of your tearful child.

Make sure your household first-aid kit is stocked with the items suggested in the list below. Smaller kits should be kept in your car or boat. For all-day or overnight camping or hiking trips it's best to take the fully equipped kit, especially if you plan to be in a remote area.

Many commercial first-aid kits will not include all the items listed here, so if you purchase a kit, check its contents

A WELL-STOCKED FIRST-AID KIT:

Children's aspirin or non-aspirin pain reliever (per doctor)
Antihistamine—for insect stings
Calamine lotion
Rubbing alcohol
Hydrogen peroxide
Topical cortisone cream—for insect bites and rashes
Petroleum jelly
Antibacterial ointment or cream
Mild soap
First-aid reference booklet or chart
Disposable, instant-activating ice bag
Thermometers—both oral and rectal
Sharp scissors with rounded tips
Tweezers
Safety pins
Sharp needles
Matches
Tongue depressors
Triangular bandage
Elastic wraps
Tourniquet
Adhesive strips of varying sizes—including butterfly bandages
Gauze rolls—varying in size from ½ to 2 inches wide
Gauze pads—2 × 2-inch and 4 × 4-inch sizes
Adhesive tape
Absorbent cotton
Cotton-tipped swabs

carefully and supplement it with the missing items—and make it a point to replace depleted items right away.

Store your first-aid kit where it will be out of your young child's reach but easily accessible. Make sure that your babysitter and older family members know where it is kept and how to administer simple first aid.

First Aid and CPR Instruction

It's a very good idea for every parent to take a course in first aid and CPR.

First-aid instruction teaches you how to react in an urgent, non–life-threatening situation such as a cut, bump, or broken bone. You will be taught what you can handle yourself, what emergencies require professional medical assistance, and what you can do until help arrives.

CPR (cardiopulmonary resuscitation) teaches you how to restore breathing and resuscitate the heart. This training could save your child's life in the crucial minutes after a serious accident.

Check with your local chapter of the American Heart Association, the American Red Cross, or your doctor or hospital to find out where these courses are offered. In many communities they are available free of charge or for a very small fee.

First-Aid Books and Charts

A first-aid handbook is essential for every household with children—and some books are directed specifically at childhood injuries. The best books contain simple, easy-to-read instructions and illustrations and cover all the common childhood first-aid remedies for everything from slivers and stings to broken bones. For recommendations about specific books, charts, and pamphlets, refer to Appendixes D and E.

Know Who and How to Call for Help

As mentioned in other parts of this book, it is very important that you keep an emergency phone list next to every phone in your home, or at least near one phone on each floor of your home. Make sure the list can be easily read by you, your older family members, visitors, and babysitters.

The list should include the phone numbers of your doctor or pediatrician, and your closest emergency hospital or paramedics. When you call, you should give your name, address, and phone number first. This way, if you are interrupted during the call, the help you have called will know where to find you. If it is an emergency situation, don't hang up before you're sure the people you have called for help have all the facts they need. Stay on the line until they indicate they are hanging up and help is on the way.

11

Poisons

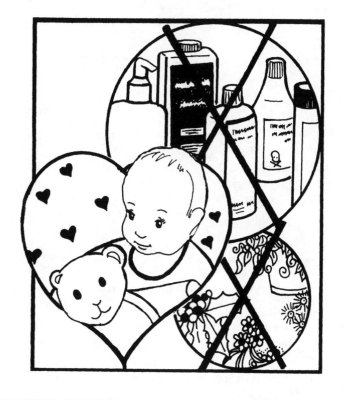

Many innocent-looking things can be harmful to your child, and many things are harmless until taken in excess

IN THIS CHAPTER we will cover how to recognize poisonous plants and household products, what to do to avoid poisoning, how to be prepared in case a poisoning occurs, and who and how to call for help and advice in an emergency.

For purposes of definition, a *poison* is any substance that can cause injury, illness, or death. Poisons can be swallowed, inhaled, or absorbed through the skin. When you consider the things that are poisonous or potentially poisonous to your child, you must erase the old images called to mind by the word "poison." It's not a simple matter of avoiding poisonous snakes and berries and locking up the drain cleaner and bug spray. Many innocent-looking things can be harmful to your child—such as the pretty lily of the valley flower. And many things are innocent until taken in excess—such as a bottle of colorful children's vitamins with iron.

In Appendixes A and B of this book, respectively, you will find lists of toxic house and garden plants and trees, and the most common household products that can be harmful to your child. Study these lists carefully and act immediately to remove them from your home or to make them off-limits to your child.

Harmful Household Products

In most cases, children are poisoned because they are curious and because they can't resist putting things into their mouths. In other cases, they are hungry and the medicine looks like candy or the liquid cleaner looks like juice. Sometimes children are poisoned when they try to imitate their parents—they see their parents taking vitamins in the morning or having a drink in the evening. But now that you are aware of the many poison hazards in your home and the incentives that move your child to get at these products, it will be easier for you to protect him.

Start your poison-protection campaign by going through your entire house, yard, porch, and garage. Identify all the potentially harmful products and centralize them. In other words, put all the garden and automotive products together in a safe place in the garage or garden shed; gather up all your cleaning supplies and locate them in one cupboard in the kitchen or storage closet. Make sure that the location is lockable and, if possible, up high out of reach.

When it comes to poisons, you should use a combination of three of the following safeguards:

- Locked room, up high, child-resistant caps
- Safety-latched or locked cabinet
- Locked shed
- Locked garage

With triple protection you leave room for human error. If a family member forgets to lock a room or re-latch a cabinet, you'll still have a backup. While you should *never* rely on child-resistant caps alone for your child's protection, it's very important to make it a rule to purchase only those products that have child-resistant caps—because those caps are your final backup should all else fail.

Poison-Prevention Tips

Aside from identifying and locking up your poisonous products, here are other things you can do (or should not do) that will help prevent accidental poisoning:

- Keep all products in their original containers. Never store harmful products in food or drink containers.
- Keep the labels on all medicines and harmful products and always use any safety closures that have been provided with the container.
- Discard all old medicines and other dangerous products by flushing them down the toilet and washing out the containers. Products that cannot be put down the toilet should be discarded in a safe trash container outside your home to which your child does not have access.
- Avoid taking medicines and vitamins in front of your young child.

- Never tell your child that a vitamin or medicine is candy, and don't buy candy for your child that resembles medicine.
- Never leave the room or yard when you are using toxic products that your child could reach. When these products are out and being used you must pay close attention to your child.
- Always read labels carefully before using products or giving them to your child.
- *Don't trust child-resistant caps.* When manufacturers test their caps, federal regulations consider 85 percent a passing grade—which means that 15 percent of the children tested may be able to open it. Also, the Consumer Product Safety Commission did a study and found that in 65 percent of the cases where children consumed medicine stored in child-resistant containers, the caps were broken or defective. The other 35 percent of the cases occurred because the lids were not tightened properly by adults.
- Don't purchase cleaning products that have spicy or fruity scents. Your child could be attracted by the smell and think it is food.
- Never allow your child to play with an empty container that once contained a harmful product.
- The leading cause of childhood poisoning is children's vitamins with iron. Iron is a dangerous toxin if taken in excess. Children's vitamins are usually pleasantly flavored, and their flavor combined with parental encouragement to "take your vitamins" makes them very appealing to children. Make sure to keep them out of your child's reach at all times and carefully monitor their use.
- Teach your child not to drink or eat anything unless it is given to her by a familiar adult, and never to take medicine given to her by schoolmates or playmates.
- When you have house guests, tell them about the precautions and safety devices you are using and remind

them to keep their medicines, tobacco, and personal-hygiene products safely out of your child's reach.

- When visiting friends and relatives, don't allow your child to wander around unless you are certain there is nothing dangerous within reach. Be extra careful when visiting grandparents because they very often have medicines and other dangerous products with easy-open caps for their own ease of use.

- Have your tap water tested to make sure it's lead free. Most copper household pipes were soldered with lead before 1986, and public water systems built before 1900 may still have lead water mains. Water running through these pipes could leach lead into your water supply.

- If your home was built before 1974, have the interior and exterior paint checked to make sure it is not lead paint. If it is, keep in mind that sanding and scraping lead paint will create dust that can cause lead poisoning in both children and adults. For information about removing lead paint, contact the Commission of Public Health listed in Appendix E, page 260.

House and Garden Plants

House and garden plants are a beautiful addition to any home. What most parents don't know is that many common house and garden plants can harm their child. Some portions of a plant, if not the whole plant, can be extremely toxic and therefore dangerous.

Make a tour of your home and yard and identify each and every plant and tree. As you identify them, refer to the list in Appendix A to see if some are listed as toxic or potentially harmful. If you find some that are, remove these from your home entirely. Keep in mind that children are natural climbers and that even a hanging plant drops its leaves from time to time, so don't take any chances.

If you identify a plant that is not listed in this book, do not assume that it is safe. Contact the nearest Poison Control Center and ask them for information. You will find a listing of the National Poison Centers in Appendix C. Don't hesitate to call them. These Poison Centers are staffed with trained professionals who are eager to answer any questions you may have.

Even safe plants can cause tummyaches or unexpected reactions in certain individuals. So when you decide to keep certain plants because you have determined they are safe, these plants should be kept out of your child's reach. Make sure that any streamers coming down from the plants are also out of reach. Write the name of each plant on the plant container so you will have quick and accurate indentification should you need it. Common names are often inaccurate because some plants have several names or the same name may be used for several closely related plants, so it's best to use both the botanical name and the common name of the plant.

As your child grows old enough to understand, teach him never to eat any part of a plant or tree unless an adult has identified it and knows that it is safe. Leaves, stalks, twigs, seeds, beans, berries, bulbs, and wild mushrooms all could be dangerous. Also teach him to recognize poison oak, poison ivy, and poison sumac and to avoid any contact with them.

Be Prepared

It is very important that you be prepared for the possibility that your child may swallow or otherwise come in contact with a poison, and this preparation should extend to other family members and babysitters:

- Post the phone numbers of your family doctor and the nearest Poison Control Center by each phone in your home or at least at one phone on each floor. Also carry this information in your purse or wallet, in case a poisoning occurs while away from home. For easy reference, a list of member hospitals of the National Poison Center Network is included as Appendix C of this book, or you may call 1-800-POISON for information about the Poison Control Center nearest you. Each center is staffed 24 hours a day by medical professionals trained to deal promptly with a poison emergency.

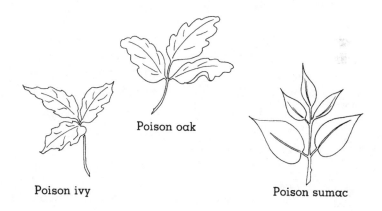

Poison oak

Poison ivy

Poison sumac

- Also keep handy, or post along with the phone numbers, the age and weight of each of your children. Remember that while you may know this by heart, you could forget it during an emergency. Or if an emergency occurs while you are gone, the babysitter or other family member may need this information.
- Keep a poison first-aid kit in your home, or at least make sure that you have a bottle of syrup of ipecac on hand. A complete poison kit contains ipecac syrup and activated charcoal. Ipecac brings on vomiting, while charcoal acts as an absorbent. When you travel, take a complete kit with you. Check the label for an expiration date and replace any item as soon as it expires.
- Read the following section carefully to be prepared for an actual poisoning emergency. Consider taking a

Poison first-aid kit

course in CPR (cardiopulmonary resuscitation) or ask your pediatrician to show you the correct way to give CPR to your child, should it ever be necessary.

If a Poisoning Occurs

If your child swallows, inhales, or comes into contact with a toxic or poisonous substance, your immediate actions will be critical for minimizing the harmful effects and maximizing her chances of complete recovery.

- Inhaled Poison: Get your child to fresh air immediately or open the doors and windows wide. Then call for help.
- Poison on the Skin: Remove any contaminated clothing and flood the skin with lukewarm water for 10 minutes.
- Swallowed Poison: If your child has swallowed medicine, don't give her anything by mouth. Call for help immediately. If she has swallowed a chemical or household product, give her water or milk immediately (unless she cannot swallow) and call for help.

Never induce vomiting (that is, never use syrup of ipecac, or any other means) unless you have been instructed to do so by your doctor, hospital, or Poison Control Center. Hydrocarbons and Petroleum Distillates can harm the respiratory system if brought back up, and some products can burn the stomach, esophagus, and throat if regurgitated.

Under no circumstances should you give your child the antidotes of ipecac syrup or activated charcoal without first contacting the Poison Control Center near you or your doctor or hospital. The two antidotes work in different ways and should be used only for certain poisons and in certain situations.

Remember:

1. Stay calm. When you call for help it is very important that you be clear and concise.
2. Call for help. If your child has swallowed a medicine or household product, or has splashed a poison in his eyes or on his skin, don't wait to see what the effects may be. Call the nearest Poison Control Center immediately. Never follow the antidote instructions on the product's label because they may be wrong or not specific enough.
3. Be ready to give the Poison Control Center:
   - Your child's age and weight
   - Your address and telephone number
   - The name of the product or medicine and the approximate amount taken (take the container to the phone with you)
   - The name and location of your nearest hospital

4. Follow their instructions precisely. The Poison Control Centers are staffed with professionals who know what's best for your child. Answer their questions accurately and clearly and follow their advice carefully. If you are instructed to take your child to a hospital, make sure to take the plant or the container that held the product or medicine with you.

Safety Outside
Your Home

12

Yard Safety

When you're very young, getting around the yard must
seem like riding the range

IN THOSE EARLY years, it
must seem like riding the range. When your child is less
than 2 years old, the yard is a lot of territory to explore. And
with a newfound ability to walk, her speed in getting away
from you may be alarming. That speed combined with the

old habit of putting everything in her mouth to test its properties makes your yard interesting and fascinating to your child, and worthy of your careful attention for safety's sake. The general rules for the yard are:

1. Don't leave your child alone in the yard. From infancy until about age 2 he'll try to eat whatever he finds there (ugh!), and from ages 2 to 4 he'll still need supervision from a close distance.
2. Fence in the yard area. If this is not possible, follow the rule of not allowing your toddler to play in an unfenced area where there is access to a street, driveway, or other hazards. Even if you are there, always remember that children can move alarmingly fast— and almost always *away* from you.
3. Investigate your yard area and follow the simple safety rules and procedures listed in this chapter.

Inspect Your Yard

While your child is still an infant you should begin your inspection of the yard to make sure all is in order and that you have done everything you can to ensure safety. In other words, get out there before the action starts: Your peace of mind will make you glad you started early.

Start by taking a walk around the exterior of your home and use the following safety checklist:

- Inspect all the wood and aluminum surfaces of your house. Watch out for peeling paint. Check for loose siding or boards, especially on porches, railings, and stairs. Make sure there are no exposed nails or screws. Also watch for torn screens, cracked or broken windows, and insect nests.

- Inspect the walkways for cracked or broken surfaces that could be a tripping hazard. During the winter, keep the walkways well salted and free of ice and snow.
- If you have window wells around your basement windows, arrange to have barriers installed. Plastic window-well guards, available at many hardware or garden stores, are very easy to install.
- Check your lawn furniture and decking for rough surfaces that could cause splinters and for exposed nails or screws. If you know or suspect that any of these items has been treated with a wood preservative, remove the item or give it two or three coats of shellac or some other sealant. The most commonly used wood preservatives are very toxic so your child should not come in contact with wood that has been treated with one.
- Lock your garbage pails in an enclosed area—in a garage or in a tool shed—someplace where they will be strictly off-limits to your child.
- If you have a woodpile located where your child will have access to it, make sure there are no termites, carpenter ants, bees, hornets, or wasps living there. And don't save boards that have nails in them.
- If you have a clothesline in your yard, see that the lines are stretched tight and are high enough that your child cannot reach them and remove any excess dangling line.
- Check the entire yard area regularly and clean up broken glass, cigarette or cigar butts, sharp metal or stone objects, pet droppings, and branches and twigs. Pay particular attention in and around your child's play area. If you have a bird feeder, put it away until your child is old enough to know not to eat the birdseed, or restrict your child from that area of the yard. Also fill any holes or deep indentations in the ground to reduce tripping hazards.

- Take an inventory of all the plants, flowers, and trees in your yard. Identify each one and check for them on the list of harmful plants in Appendix A. If you find that some are listed as harmful, remove them or restrict your child from that area of the yard. Remember that some thorny plants, though not harmful, could be hurtful.
- Inspect all outdoor electrical outlets to make sure they are ground fault circuit interrupter (GFCI) outlets, which will help protect your family from possible electric shock. See Chapter 2 for more information about this type of outlet. Also make sure every outlet has a safety cover.

Inspecting your yard as suggested above is a good starting point for safety. You may even find a few other small repairs that you just haven't gotten around to doing, and now, with your approaching toddler/explorer soon to make the scene, those little repairs are in order.

Fences

If you don't have a fenced-in yard or play area, consider creating one, especially if your family enjoys the outdoor features of your home. A fence will not only help prevent your child from wandering out of the yard but will also help keep out unwanted visitors and pets. The most important rule about fences is that you should not allow the fence to give you a false sense of security. Many children find the challenge of climbing fences irresistible.

If you are currently in the market for a new fence, select a style that is difficult or impossible for a small child to climb over, under, or through. If you are considering a wooden fence, select one that has straight or rounded boards across the top and boards that are sanded smooth to avoid splinters.

If you are considering a chain-link fence, look for one that has hooked barbs rather than twisted barbs at the top and bottom.

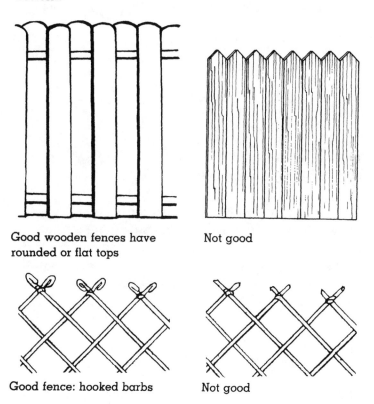

Good wooden fences have
rounded or flat tops

Not good

Good fence: hooked barbs

Not good

FENCE SAFETY TIPS

- See that the gate is self-closing and self-locking and that the lock is high enough (at least 50 inches from the ground) so that it cannot be reached by a 2-year-old. Check the hinges often to make sure they are not loose. Never allow your small child, or older children, to "swing" on the gate.
- Eliminate peeling paint, splinters, rust, and loose or protruding nails. Check for these hazards on a regular basis.

- Also check regularly for loose boards and any holes in or under the fence large enough for your child to fit her head through. Small children sometimes think if their head fits, their body will too, and they could get stuck.
- If your neighbors have a dog, it may be a good idea to make sure your child cannot reach his hands or fingers through the fence.
- When your child is old enough to understand, begin instructing her about the dangers associated with fence climbing and rough play near fences. Most accidents concerning fences involve climbing, falling off, or falling against the fence during play.

Completion of your fenced-in area means that you have defined your basic play area for toddler-proofing purposes.

Backyard play equipment for toddlers frequently means a swing set or play gym, often a sandbox, and even a swimming pool. We'll discuss these next.

Swing Sets and Play Yards

In the typical "toddler-type" backyard, the first thing that comes to mind is the traditional swing set. It seems that good ideas never become outdated, and swing sets and play yards have given children hours of fun and entertainment for generations. If you are adding a swing set/play yard for your child, a few general safety rules apply.

- All playground equipment should be installed over yielding surfaces such as sand, sawdust, wood chips, or bark; the ground surface should be level; and the equipment should be located at least six feet from the nearest obstruction (fence, house, etc.).

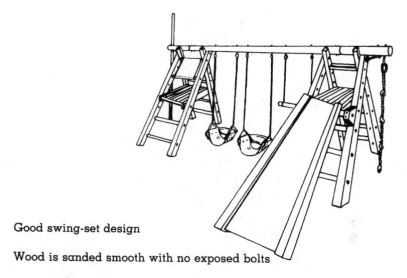

Good swing-set design

Wood is sanded smooth with no exposed bolts

U-shaped swings firmly anchored

- The equipment you select should be sturdy and safe and carefully assembled. Make sure wood is sanded smoothly to avoid scratches or splinters. There should be no exposed screws or bolts. Avoid equipment that has **S**-hooks as fasteners or holders because these can catch clothing. Do not select equipment with rings between 5 and 10 inches in diameter because these can entrap a child's head.
- The equipment should be firmly anchored. Assume that your child will try to swing higher than he should and sink the support posts of a swing set into cement footings. This is the only foolproof way to prevent a swing set from tipping.
- Select equipment with heavy plastic or rubber **U**-shaped seats. The best **U**-shaped seat has an extra strap around the back of the seat to help keep a child from falling over backwards. For your very young child, special safety swings are available that have a safety bar and crotch strap to keep your baby safely sitting while

you push the swing. It's a good idea to select one of these safe swing designs.

Safe swing designs

- Check the play equipment periodically for loose hardware and missing screw or bolt caps.

SAFETY RULES FOR SWING-SET AND PLAY-YARD USE

Once your swing set has been safely installed, you are now ready to begin supervised toddler use.

THE BIG RULE FOR SWING-SET AND
PLAY-YARD USE:

Until your child is old enough and has mastered all
the necessary skills of coordination and balance, he
should have adult supervision at all times when
using a swing set or any kind of playground equipment. If you teach and enforce the following safety
rules in your own backyard, as your child grows he
will take what he has learned to the playgrounds
where the "big kids" play.

Memorize these rules for use of playground equipment
so that you can teach your child safety as well as fun:

Swing Rules

- No kneeling or standing on swings
- Stop the swing before getting off
- Don't walk directly in front of or behind a moving swing
- Hold on with both hands
- Never twist a swing, or swing an empty swing
- No swinging "double"
- Don't swing too high
- Never push someone in a swing who isn't expecting it

Slide Rules

- Check to see if the slide is hot before sliding
- Don't climb up the slide the wrong way
- Don't slide down if someone is still on the slide
- Don't slide down if someone is standing at the bottom
- No sliding "double"
- No sliding head first, backwards, sideways, or with legs
  folded

- Leave the bottom of the slide quickly

Monkey-Bar Rules

- No climbing on wet bars
- Always use both hands at all times
- Watch for other children before swinging your feet
- Watch for others swinging their feet
- Never jump off; climb down carefully
- Never use monkey bars mounted on concrete or asphalt

Teeter-Totter Rules

- Both children must get on and off together
- No riding "double"
- No riding backwards or sideways
- Never straddle the board with your feet under the board
- Hold on with both hands at all times
- No standing or walking across the board

Always remember that your swing set or play yard, safely installed and used, will provide hours of enjoyment for your little one.

Sandboxes

Children can have hours of creative fun playing in the sand. Just to make sure your child isn't digging for trouble, take a few precautions:

- Make sure your sandbox has a cover that can keep out dogs, cats, and other animals. A cover will also keep the sand dry.
- Check the sand often for sharp or rusty objects that may have become buried there by accident or for "safe-keeping." A sand sifter would be very handy for this,

but the best do-it-yourself device is a piece of window screen.

- Replace the sand at least once a year. Purchase sand that has been specially intended for play and avoid white, powdery sands made from crushed rock, especially marble. This is a controversial issue right now, but some scientists maintain that this white, powdery sand may contain carcinogens. Find out where the sand came from and select sand that is natural rather than manufactured. Natural sand is generally a light tan color and a little coarser, rather than powdery and white.

Swimming-Pool Safety

Today, swimming pools, in one version or another—the small plastic wading pool, the aboveground semipermanent structure, or the full in-ground permanent pool—are affordable by many households with toddlers.

The big rule for any type of pool calls for *supervision*.

Never leave your infant or small child alone near the pool for even a second, even if your child is wearing a life jacket or you feel she is a fair swimmer. If you have to leave the pool area, take your child with you.

You might consider purchasing a portable telephone when you buy even a wading pool. When the phone rings, you'll be able to answer it right there without taking your attention away from your child. (Keep emergency telephone numbers handy here as well.)

Always remember that wading pools must be emptied after each use, and that aboveground or in-ground pools must be fenced in on all sides with barriers that are difficult to climb and gates that lock securely. Ask your insurance agent for details about local laws governing pool fencing and what your insurance company recommends as the safest possible fencing for your particular type of pool.

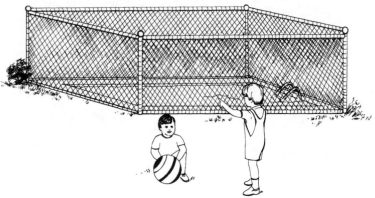

All pools except waders must be completely fenced in

RULES FOR ALL SWIMMING POOLS

Regardless of the type of swimming pool you have, keep the following rules in mind:

- Have a telephone at poolside to avoid having to leave your child unattended in or near the pool to answer the phone elsewhere. Keep emergency phone numbers at the poolside telephone.
- Do not allow your children (or adults, for that matter) to use the pool if there is lightning around (even in the distance) or a thunderstorm is threatening.
- Always test the temperature of the water before you take your small baby into a pool. Make sure the temperature is at least 80°F.
- Don't allow other children or adults to splash the water or make big waves near your small infant.
- When children are playing in water they can tire rather

quickly. Insist on rest breaks every half-hour for children under 5 years old. Watch for these indications of fatigue: chills, dizziness, weakness, frequent loss of balance, or a purplish color to lips or fingernails. These are signs that it's time for a rest break.

RULES FOR LARGER SWIMMING POOLS

If you are planning for the installation and use of a large pool, either aboveground or built in, be very careful to see that it is installed in accordance with local codes and regulations, and that your insurance agent's recommendations have been followed. Some rules for the use of larger pools:

- If you use a pool cover, do not consider it a substitute for fencing or supervision and always make sure to keep it clear of rainwater and pool water. Never allow your child to climb on the pool cover while it's on the pool.
- See that all exit doors from the house to the pool are routinely kept locked and that the lock is placed at a height of at least 5 feet.
- Do not locate yard furniture outside the pool fence where it could be used as an aid to fence climbing.
- If there are bushes and trees near the pool, keep them trimmed in order to maintain a clear view of the pool from the house so that trespassers can be seen.
- Keep toys away from the pool area because a young child playing with the toys could accidentally fall in the water.
- Remove steps to an aboveground pool when not in use.
- Install a float line across the pool to indicate where the deep water begins. This will help prevent your child from unconsciously venturing into deeper water.
- Electrical equipment such as radios and gardening tools must be kept at a safe distance from the pool so

they cannot be accidentally dropped or pushed into the water.

Make sure that infants and children always use a life jacket if they have not mastered swimming

- Always insist that infants and children wear life jackets if they are near a pool and have not yet mastered swimming. When selecting life jackets, make sure the label says they are Coast Guard approved and that the weight limits on the jacket correspond with the weight of the child who will be wearing it. There are even special life jackets for infants.
- Do not allow your child to use inflatable toys and rafts in water over his head unless he is a good swimmer or he is wearing a life jacket.
- If your child is under 5 years of age, do not allow her to use fins, face masks, or water slides.
- As an additional safety precaution, you might consider purchasing a battery-operated pool alarm. This alarm floats in the water and detects disturbances to the surface; if a person or pet falls in the water, it emits a loud warning sound. The best pool alarms are equipped with a remote receiver so that the alarm will sound at poolside and on the remote receiver simultaneously. If you do install such a device, remember that it is *not* a substitute for secure fencing or parental supervision.

Battery-operated pool alarm

SWIMMING RULES TO TEACH YOUR CHILD

As your child grows, learns to swim, and begins to enjoy the facilities of a large pool, proper and safe poolside behavior becomes quite important. These rules should be applied to every pool, not just your own:

- No swimming alone
- No swimming with long hair that is not tied back
- No running on pool deck or diving board
- No pushing or kicking—on the deck or in the pool
- No tickling in the pool
- No diving into inner tubes or jumping onto other inflatables
- No dunking
- No riding "double" on the water slide
- No glass allowed in pool area
- No playing near drains or other pool fittings
- No diving near other swimmers
- No diving backwards
- No diving from the sides of the pool
- No diving from the sides of the diving board
- No diving of any kind in an aboveground pool

Spas and hot tubs can present a threat of drowning or overheating. Your young child under 5 years old should be excluded from their use.

And one last point for safety's sake: Whether your pool is an aboveground or in-ground pool, it is most advisable that you take a course in CPR (cardiopulmonary resuscitation). These classes are likely to be offered free or at low cost at your local Red Cross, YMCA, YWCA, or any other organization involved in recreational safety. If you have difficulty in locating a class, ask your family doctor for suggestions.

Other Areas of Your Yard

The portions of the yard just discussed focus on play areas for you and your infant or toddler. However, it's also easy to imagine your little one outside when someone is mowing the lawn, cooking on the barbecue, or just doing a little gardening.

LAWN-MOWING SAFETY

Whenever it's time to mow the lawn, your children should not be allowed out in the yard. Most power lawn mowers have rotary blades that can reach speeds of more than 200 miles per hour, and because of this power they can propel things like rocks and twigs more than 50 feet through the air at incredible speed. Grass trimmers that use the "whip" method, leaf blowers, and snow blowers can also throw debris considerable distances. Make it a strict rule that no children or pets will be out in the yard when these powerful machines are being used.

BARBECUE SAFETY

When you're cooking outdoors, make sure your child cannot get anywhere near the barbecue grill. Remember that the outside surface of the grill becomes intensely hot while you're cooking and remains hot for quite some time afterward. If you are cooking with charcoal, the embers can stay red-hot for hours.

You may want to consider installing a portable area enclosure around the barbecue or keep your child in a playpen or portable play area if you want him in the yard with you while you are cooking. Locate the playpen or play area away from the direction of the smoke. When you are finished cooking, make sure to clear away all barbecue equipment such as fire starters, charcoal, forks, tongs, and dishes.

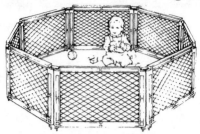

Portable play areas provide outdoor protection

GARAGE, TOOL SHED, AND GARDEN SHED

These three areas should be made completely off-limits to your young children. Almost every item stored in these places is a potential danger to your child.

The following is a list of items that should never be left out in the yard or driveway—they should always be locked up securely in the garage, tool shed, or gardening shed.

ALWAYS LOCK THESE ITEMS UP:

Gardening and lawn-care tools and machinery
Carpentry tools and machinery
Barbecue equipment, charcoal, lighter fluids
Pesticides and insecticides
Fertilizers and weed killers
Car-care products, including polish, antifreeze, and oil
Painting and wood-finishing products
Alcohol, gasoline, kerosene, and turpentine
Flower seeds and bulbs
Birdseed and pet foods
Ladders and step stools
Hoses and sprinklers

Plug locks help protect
dangerous power tools

You should take extra precautions in these areas, just in
case your child should happen
to find her way into your garage
or shed. Store all harmful products up high on shelves or in a
locked cupboard. Keep all your
tools up high on the wall, on a
high shelf, or in a locked box or
drawer. Cover the lawn and garden equipment with a heavy
tarp and hide the ignition keys.
There are also special locks that
attach to the plugs of power
tools to prevent them from being
plugged in. These plug locks are
a good idea for dangerous power
tools such as drills, saws, and electric lawn mowers.

In these areas door security is most important. Refer to
Chapter 2 for information about the locking and latching
options available.

Check your garage door. If you have an automatic opener,
make sure that it is equipped with an automatic reverse
feature. This feature will cause the door to open again if it
encounters an object before it is fully closed. Most of the
garage-door openers built after 1982 have a more sensitive
reversing device than those made earlier. But be aware that
even equipped with this feature it is possible for the door,
especially the older models, to seriously injure a child. So
keep the remote-control devices locked safely in your glove
compartment. Also make sure the switch button in your
garage is up very high out of your child's reach, and consider
installing a safety lock switch in place of the button so that
the door cannot be activated from inside the garage without
the key.

DRIVEWAY SAFETY

Driveways are the place where many accidents can happen, but if you follow the safety tips listed below you will be eliminating the major dangers associated with this area.

- Never back out of the garage without first checking to see that there are no children or childen's toys in the driveway behind or under the car and always back up slowly.
- Do not allow your child to play in the car, even when it is parked in the driveway. Even a parked car is unsafe for children. Keep the doors of your car locked at all times just to be safe.
- Keep your driveway free from oil, antifreeze, and gasoline spots. Remember, if it's there, your child will be sure to find it.

13

Playing It Safe Outdoors

As your child marches into the great outdoors, he confronts the sun, heat, bugs, water, and snow

WHEN YOUR LITTLE one is first born, his needs are fairly basic and somewhat rudimentary in nature. As the saying goes, time flies, and as he marches into his toddler years his interest in the great outdoors increases dramatically. Look at it this way: He may want to put on his helmet, mount his tricycle, use roller skates, travel by sled, toboggan, or snow disk, and confront the sun, heat, bugs, water, and snow!

Sun Safety

To begin, let's consider a simple element—the sun. It's likely this will be one of the first safety considerations of the great outdoors, because it's easy for you and your infant to enjoy the sun in your own backyard. The first thing to remember, though, is that your baby's skin is very delicate and sensitive, and because of this it is very important that you protect her from overexposure to the sun. Even five minutes of sun at the wrong time of the day could be unhealthy for your baby. The best rule is to keep your child out of direct sun during her first year.

Keep your child out of direct sun during her first year

For those of you who are "sun worshippers," and are determined to sun your baby as well, wait until she is at least 9 months old. Then begin sunning by allowing her only two minutes of sun each day on her front and two minutes on her back. Gradually increase the time over a month to about 40 minutes of total sun time—20 minutes on each side.

The sun's rays are most intense between 10 A.M. and 2 P.M. during standard time and between 11 A.M. and 3 P.M. during daylight saving time. Never directly expose your child to this midday sun until she is at least 2 years old. Arrange sunning time for before 10:00 A.M. and after 3:00 P.M. When your child is about 2 years old, she will be able to endure more sun. But you should still avoid exposing her to the sun from 11 A.M. to 2 P.M. and make sure to use sunscreens liberally, especially if she is fair-skinned with blond or red hair and light eyes. Remember that no sunscreen will prevent burning if your child is out in the sun too long, and if she is playing in the water or perspiring, the sunscreen will wash off and should be reapplied more frequently.

ABOUT SUNSCREENS

Sunscreen lotions and ointments contain substances that filter out the damaging rays of the sun and are an important element of your sun-protection program. The higher the Sun Protection Factor (SPF), the greater the protection.

Sunblocks are not recommended if your baby is under 6 months old. When your child is over 6 months old, select a sunscreen that is rated at SPF 15 or higher and is waterproof. Also select one that is PABA-free, because PABA has been known to cause allergic reactions in some children.

TIPS ON SUNSCREENS

- For your baby or young child, select a sunscreen that is a milky lotion or cream. These are more soothing than clear lotions and it is easier to see where you have applied it.
- Apply the sunscreen 15 to 30 minutes before exposure to the sun in order to allow it to penetrate the lower

layers of the skin. Reapply it liberally and frequently—
every 60 to 90 minutes.

- Be careful when applying sunscreens around the eye area because children tend to rub their eyes.
- Use a sunblock stick or balm for extra-sensitive areas such as the lips, nose, and ears.

TIPS ON SUN EXPOSURE

These rules apply, for casual sunning or incidental sun exposure, as well as for trips to the beach:

- Don't be fooled by cloudy skies. As much as 80 percent of the sun's rays still reach the earth even when the sky is overcast.
- Beware of reflected light. Many surfaces like sand, snow, cement, water, or light-colored walls and buildings can reflect harmful rays from the sun. Because your child is sitting in the shade or under an umbrella does not guarantee he is protected from the sun. Take extra care by covering your child with protective lightweight clothing and by using a sunscreen.
- Ask your doctor if any medication your child may be taking could increase her sensitivity to sunlight.
- Be particularly careful at high altitudes. For every 1,000 feet above sea level, radiation increases 4 or 5 percent. Also, the closer you are to the equator, the stronger the sun's rays become. So take extra care when you visit warm climates or areas high in the mountains.
- Cover up your baby with a sun hat, a long-sleeved shirt, and long pants. Select light-colored fabrics that are tightly woven or double the layers.

TEACH YOUR CHILD ABOUT SUN SAFETY

An effective sun-protection program goes beyond the occasional weekend trip to the beach. You should teach your child good sun-protection habits in the same way you are teaching other safety and health habits. Your child needs to learn to protect himself from the sun in all climates and during all activities—playing sports, shoveling snow, walking to school, having a picnic, mowing the lawn, or anything else outside.

The Heat of the Day

With a little age and mobility, your little one will end up expending tremendous amounts of energy in her play—right through the heat of the day!

When children play long and vigorously in the heat they can sometimes develop signs of heat exhaustion—heat cramps, faintness, and even total collapse. Children seem to be more susceptible to this than adults because they lose more body water faster and they very often ignore the signals of discomfort to slow down. Follow these simple steps to avoid heat exhaustion:

- Don't allow your child to play vigorously in temperatures over 90°F. When the temperature is this high it is best to encourage your child to find indoor activities of a quiet nature. Be particularly careful on days that are humid and windless.
- Make sure your child drinks plenty of cool water before, during, and after play. Teach your child that cool water is the ideal beverage and try to avoid drinks that contain sugar when the purpose is to quench thirst and replace body fluids lost through perspiration. Even in moderately hot weather, schedule rest periods for cooling off and quenching thirst.

- Remember that a child can suffer heat stress even if he is not running or playing hard. So never leave your child in a room that is especially hot or in an unattended car—even if the windows are open. The temperature in a parked car can reach as high as 130°F in a matter of minutes if the sun is shining on it.

Beating the Bugs

In warmer climates and during the warm-weather months in the northern climates there are thousands of insects around—on the water, in the grass, flying through the air. Most of these bugs are completely harmless to humans, but there are some that can be irritating or even dangerous to your small child.

The best thing you can do for your child to prevent exposure to these insects is to follow these guidelines:

- Always make sure your child is wearing long pants, long sleeves, and shoes and socks when she is in an area where she may be exposed to many insects. Avoid bright-colored clothing and scented shampoos or soaps.
- Check your own backyard often to see that it is free of insect nests, anthills, stagnant water that may attract mosquitoes, etc. Keep your lawn mowed to a short length, to help keep the insect population down too.
- If your child will be in an area where insects are unavoidable, apply an insect repellent to his clothing and any exposed skin. Check with your doctor for recommendations on which repellent to use for your child because some repellents are too strong for small children. DEET (diethyl toluamide) is generally considered the most effective ingredient. Never allow your child to spray himself: Spray it into the palm of your hand first and then apply it to his skin, avoiding the areas

around the eyes and mouth. You should only use a repellent on your small child when absolutely necessary—repeated applications have been known to cause allergic reactions in some children, especially infants.

TREATING BITES AND STINGS

If your child suffers a bug bite or sting in spite of all your efforts, the first-aid treatment chart on pages 206 and 207 will help you alleviate the itching or pain, and decide when to call your doctor. If you are not sure what type of insect was responsible for the bite or sting, watch closely for dangerous symptoms such as hives, swelling all over the body, difficulty breathing, fever, stomach upset, spreading rash, or a stung area that remains red for more than two days. If your child shows any of these symptoms, you should go to your doctor or to the emergency room for immediate treatment.

INSECT	HABITAT	SYMPTOMS	SPECIAL NOTES	TREATMENT
Mosquito	Pools, lakes, bird-baths, standing water	Stinging sensation followed by small, red, itchy mound with tiny puncture marks at the center	Mosquitos are attracted by bright colors, sweat, and sweet odors such as perfumes, scented soaps, and shampoos	Cold compresses and calamine lotion (except near eyes or genitals)
Fly	Food, garbage, animal waste	Painful, itchy bumps; may turn into small blisters	Bites often disappear in a day but may last longer	As above
Flea	Rugs, pet hair, cracks in floors	Small bump that looks like a hive; often in groups where clothes fit tightly (waist, buttocks)	Most likely to be a problem in homes with pets	Calamine lotion

Bedbug	Cracks in walls or floors; crevices of furniture; bedding	Itchy red bumps surrounded by a blister; usually two or three in a row	Most likely to bite at night, but victim may not awaken; less active during cold weather	Cleansing with soap; calamine lotion
Fire Ant	Builds mounds in pastures, meadows, lawns, and parks	Immediate pain and burning; swelling up to ½ inch; cloudy fluid in area of bite	Fire ants usually attack intruders; some children have reactions such as difficulty in breathing, fever, and stomach upset	Cold compresses, cool baths, calamine lotion, topical cortisone cream. *Severe reactions:* consult M.D. immediately
Bee, Wasp, and Yellow Jacket	Flowers, shrubs, picnic areas, beaches	Immediate pain and rapid swelling	A few children have severe reactions such as difficulty in breathing and swelling all over the body; go to the emergency room	As above. Oral antihistamine if very itchy; bee-sting kit if allergic. To remove stinger, do not squeeze with forceps—scrape horizontally across stinger with forceps or credit card
Tick	Woods and grassy fields	May be hidden in hair or on skin	Don't remove by using match, lighter, cigarette, or nail-polish remover	Grasp tick's body near head with forceps and pull firmly and steadily; don't leave any parts under the skin. Consult M.D. Bring the tick if possible.

Water Safety Away from Home

If you practice good water safety while your child is young, as a result of your good example your child will grow up with a healthy respect for water, knowledge of its hidden dangers, and an appreciation of its many pleasures.

The water is one place where there must be constant eye-contact adult supervision. Do not allow your child of any age to swim alone or unsupervised. It is best to take your child where there is a professionally trained lifeguard on duty. Follow the pool, beach, or waterfront rules and teach your child to do the same.

SAFETY TIPS FOR POOLS AWAY FROM HOME

Pool safety in your own backyard is discussed in Chapter 12, and those safety guidelines should be followed both at home and away. Plus the points about lifeguards in the next section on beach tips apply here as well.

SAFETY TIPS FOR THE BEACH

- If the water is too rough or deep for your small child, take along a portable pool and place it a safe distance from the water. This way your child will still have fun in the water and be safe.
- Do not visit beaches where there are no lifeguards or first-aid stations unless you or someone with you has been trained in life-saving techniques and mouth-to-mouth resuscitation. Closely supervise your child even when a lifeguard is present.
- Never leave your young child alone at a beach even if

there is a lifeguard present. Lifeguards are not intended to be babysitters.

- Don't allow your child in the water if there is a storm threatening or if there is *any* evidence of lightning or thunder, no matter how far away it seems.
- If your small child is afraid of the water because of the waves or for other reasons, don't force him to go into the water. Toddlers are easily knocked over by surf and undertow and this can be very frightening to them.
- Teach your child to call for help if she is in pain or in trouble, but never to fake a call for help.
- If your child does not know how to swim or if the water is rough or wavy, make sure he is wearing a life jacket that is Coast Guard approved for the body of water you are swimming in. Remember that no young child is "water safe" even if the child knows how to swim. Ask the lifeguard about the water conditions and potential hazards such as undertow, cross-currents, riptides, and run-outs.

All children should wear life preservers when near water

SAFETY TIPS FOR SMALL LAKES, RIVERS, CREEKS, AND PONDS

- The early spring and summer water of a river, creek, or pond can be extremely cold, and may cause cramps and breathing problems. Check the temperature of the water before you allow your child to wade or swim, and don't allow her in if it is below 60°F.
- Don't allow your child to wade barefoot. Tennis shoes will help protect his feet if he encounters broken glass or rusty cans lurking on the bottom.
- If the creek or river has a current strong enough to topple a small child or if there are areas where the bottom drops off and then suddenly becomes deep, your child should wear her life jacket—even if she is only wading.
- Don't allow your child in the water if there is a storm threatening or if there is lightning or thunder anywhere in the vicinity.
- Teach your child never to swim in areas where there are fishing lines or motor boats and never to dive or jump into water of unknown depth.
- When your small child is fishing from the shore or dock and the water at the shoreline has a strong current or is over his head, he should be wearing his life jacket.
- When boating with your child or infant, make sure she is wearing her life jacket at all times—even if you're only on the dock. Teach your child to stay seated at all times in a boat and position her near you in the middle of the boat, not in the bow. Avoid speeding, sharp turns, and high-traffic areas.
- Never allow your small child to board a boat ahead of anyone else. Pass him to another adult on the boat or first board yourself and then assist your child onto the boat.

- Teach your child to call for help if she is in pain or in trouble, but never to fake a call for help.

The above guidelines regarding water refer generally to your child's toddler years and up. Your care, love, and intelligent supervision at the beginning will teach your child all the right things to do—safely. And when he is ready for swimming lessons, the water around him will be a comfort, not a threat.

SWIMMING LESSONS

It is best to wait until your child is 3 years old before giving him swimming instructions. The head of a child under 3 years old is large in proportion to the rest of his body and this makes it more difficult for him to hold his head out of the water when floating horizontally.

The American Academy of Pediatrics offers the following guidelines about enrolling an infant or toddler in a swimming class: "Organized group swimming instruction for children under 3 years of age is not recommended. Learning to swim at this age does not make your child water safe. Infants and toddlers in swimming programs are at increased risk of infection and convulsions from swallowing large quantities of water. Total submersion should be prohibited and YMCA guidelines for infant swimming should be followed."

The Academy further recommends that children under 3 years of age should only be taught swimming in a properly maintained pool on a one-to-one basis by a parent or a responsible adult who is a trained instructor, and that infants with known medical problems should receive a clearance from their physician.

If you decide to give swimming instructions to your child when he is under 3 years old, remember never to consider him "water safe," no matter how skillful he appears to be in the water.

Cycling Safety

To some parents of infants, cycling safety may seem a bit premature. To other parents, this consideration is completely natural because they enjoy bicycling and look forward to taking their baby for bicycle rides. This section covers cycling safety in its natural order: child carriers for adult bicycles, tricycles, and your child's first bicycle, as well as the importance of helmets for cycling.

CHILD CARRIERS FOR ADULT BICYCLES

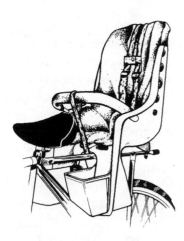

Good child carrier design

Fairly early in life, your baby can be taken for a ride on an adult bicycle. Just remember, before you start taking your baby for bike rides she must be old enough to sit up unsupported and her neck must be strong enough to support a small child's bicycle helmet. Usually a child is mature enough for this at about 9 months old.

When you're shopping for a child carrier for your bicycle, be sure to select one that has these safety features:

- A rear-mounted carrier that can be securely installed over the rear wheel. (Front carriers are not recommended because they make it much more difficult to control the bicycle.)

- Molded foot wells to keep your child's feet safe from the spokes of the bicycle.
- A high back that will help protect against neck injury and will also give your child a place to rest his head.
- A sturdy shoulder harness and lap belt that will support your child even if she falls asleep.

Once your bicycle carrier has been selected from a safety point of view, certain safety rules should be followed regarding its use:

- Your child should always wear a lightweight baby's helmet. Select a helmet that meets the ANSI or Snell standards for safety (the Snell standards are the more stringent).
- Only a competent adult cyclist should be allowed to bicycle with your baby as a passenger.
- Never bicycle with your baby on busy streets or during bad weather. Restrict your riding to parks and bicycle paths or very quiet streets.
- When your child is a passenger on your bicycle, always ride with extreme caution and at slower speeds.
  - Never leave your baby in the bicycle carrier when the bicycle is parked on the kickstand.

Safe tricycle design

TRICYCLES

Your baby can graduate to a tricycle with supervised use by the time he has learned to walk up the stairs by putting one foot in front of the other in rotation.

At this point you may be tempted to select a tricycle as you might select clothing—large enough so he can grow into it later. But this is not a good idea from a safety standpoint. In order for your child to have proper balance and control, his tricycle should be based upon his present size and ability.

To measure your child for a tricycle, first measure your child's inseam from crotch to floor (with bare feet). Then measure the tricycle from the crotch position of the seat to the most distant spot the pedals will reach. If your child's inseam measurement is as long or longer than the tricycle measurement, the tricycle is sized properly for your child.

13 ½

How to measure
your child for a tricycle

13 ½

When selecting a tricycle for your child, look for these safety features:

- Sturdy, quality construction without sharp edges or protrusions.
- A low seat and wheels that are widely spaced for improved stability and balance.
- Pedals and hand grips with rough, nonslip surfaces to help prevent little hands and feet from slipping.
- Wheels with the safer hubcap-type covers, rather than spokes.
- No rear step for riding "double."

Once your child's tricycle has been selected, remember that proper maintenance is a key factor in tricycle safety. Check your child's tricycle regularly for missing or damaged pedals and handgrips, loose handlebars and seats, or other broken or defective parts.

Certain safety rules apply to the use of the tricycle, and you should teach them to your child:

- Riding downhill is very dangerous: Tricycles can pick up speed very quickly and this can make the tricycle almost impossible to control and difficult to stop safely.
- Never make sharp turns that could cause the trike to topple over, and make all turns at a low speed.
- Don't ride a trike over curbs or down steps.
- Don't ride "double" because this can make the trike unstable and difficult to control.
- Never ride down the driveway and into the street—this has been found to be one of the biggest causes of tricycle/car accidents.
- Keep hands and feet away from moving parts of the tricycle, especially spokes.
- Always wear a cycling helmet.
- Always put the tricycle away at night to avoid rusting and weakening of metal parts.

BICYCLES

A first bicycle with training wheels and foot brakes.

Sooner or later your child will be ready to go "big time"— a bicycle! According to the American Academy of Pediatrics, this will be at about 5 or 6 years of age, and you should not encourage your child to ride a bicycle until he is ready. You must take into consideration your child's coordination and desire to learn.

When selecting a bicycle for your child it is best to take him with you so you can test the bike for proper fit. These are the rules for a good-fitting bicycle:

- Have your child sit on the seat with his hands on the handlebars. In this position he must be able to place the balls of his feet on the floor.
- If the bicycle has a center bar, have your child straddle the bar. He should be able to keep both feet flat on the floor with about two inches of clearance between his crotch and the bar.

It is best to select coaster (foot) brakes for your child's first bicycle. A bicycle with handbrakes requires much more coordination and enough strength to apply sufficient pressure to stop the bike.

When your child receives his first bicycle, he needs to be taught that the bike is not a toy and that it carries with it many responsibilities for safety. Until your child is age 7 or over, he should ride only with your supervision or that of another responsible adult, and he should not be allowed in the street. During this time you will have the opportunity to teach him the many important rules concerning bicycle safety. Refer to Appendix E for information about how to obtain free literature about safe bicycling.

CYCLING HELMETS

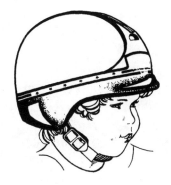

Bicycle safety helmet

Whether riding on an adult bicycle, a tricycle, or her own full-size bicycle, your child should not be without the protection of a safety helmet. The American Academy of Pediatrics, the National Safety Council, and the Bicycle Federation of America are all unconditionally in favor of cycling helmets. The biggest excuses for not wearing a helmet in the past have been looks and comfort. But today there is such a great selection of attractive and lightweight designs that those excuses don't hold up.

Studies indicate that if your child wears a helmet while cycling he will be four times less likely to suffer a head injury. So when you purchase a tricycle or bicycle for your child, get a cycling helmet as well. If you get your child used to the idea of wearing a helmet right from the start, it will be much easier.

Look for a helmet that has been approved by the Snell Memorial Foundation (the strictest standards available today) and/or the American National Standards Institute (ANSI). These helmets will offer the following features:

- A strong, smooth outer shell to help lessen the impact of a fall and to protect against sharp objects.
- An energy-absorbing liner to help absorb the impact of a fall. This liner should be at least ½ inch thick and is usually made of polystyrene, the type of foam used for picnic coolers.
- A chin strap and fastener to keep the helmet from shifting or falling off.

Select a helmet that fits your child properly. Most helmets are adjustable within a size range and are sized based on head circumference measured around the top of the forehead. Also make very sure the helmet is lightweight (less than one pound) and comfortable and will be cool in hot weather. Many of the newer designs have air vents for this purpose. Remember, your child will be more apt to put it on and keep it on if it feels comfortable to him.

Roller Skates

At the proper point in time when your child has acquired sufficient coordination, roller-skating can be good family fun. Just remember that close, hands-on supervision is absolutely necessary until your child is adept at this sport.

When purchasing or renting roller skates for your child, choose skates that fit his present shoe size, not a pair he will grow into. If there are metal parts on the skates, carefully run your hand over them to check for sharp edges and points that could cause a cut during a fall.

For beginners there are special skates that have a locking tab to inhibit the skater from rolling backward, and these tabs also slow down the forward motion so your child cannot go too fast, which helps with the problem many beginners have of the skates rolling out from under them.

SAFETY TIPS FOR ROLLER-SKATING

Again, the principal rule here is that until your child is adept at skating, your hands-on supervision will be an absolute necessity. But even though you are close at hand, there are other safety measures to make this learning experience even safer:

- Make sure your child is wearing close-fitting clothing that covers his shoulders, elbows, and knees.
- Protective elbow and knee pads and a safety helmet will help eliminate scrapes and bumps from those unavoidable spills every beginner experiences.
- Check the skating surface carefully. Avoid areas with uneven or broken cement or other obstacles such as gravel, branches, and twigs.
- Never allow your child to skate in the street or down the driveway and into the street.
- If you allow your child to skate indoors—such as in the basement or garage—check very carefully to make sure that there are no projecting nails or screws or other objects that could cause injury if your child should skate into them. Remember that when skating inside, most children reach for a wall or a nearby piece of furniture to help them stop.
- Teach your child that when outdoors, if he feels he is going to fall, he should try to land on the grass or some other nearby shock-absorbing surface. Learning how to fall is important, too. The idea is to roll onto fleshy parts of the body, such as the buttocks and upper legs, rather than land on more fragile areas such as the hands. And although it may be difficult, skaters should try to relax, rather than stiffening, when they fall.

Sleds, Toboggans, and Snow Disks

Infants and toddlers under the age of 2 should not participate in downhill sledding and tobogganing activities—even as a passenger accompanied by an adult. There are just too many safety risks involved for a fragile young child. Until your child is old enough, it is best to take her for rides by pulling her on a safety sled or snow disk on relatively level ground.

Safety sled

Once your child is old enough to participate in downhill sledding or tobogganing, she should be closely supervised by you until about the age of 6 or 7. During this time, you can teach her all the necessary safety rules concerning these sports.

SELECTING SAFE SNOW-SPORTS EQUIPMENT

- Check for sturdy construction. Avoid split or splintered wood and metal parts bent out of shape when buying secondhand equipment.

- Look for secure handholds.
- Avoid equipment with sharp, jagged edges and protruding rivets.
- Look for an energy-absorbing pad for toboggan seats.
- Check sleds for easy steering without jamming.
- Avoid sleds with runners that end in sharp-edged hooks.

SAFETY RULES FOR SNOW SPORTS

- Look over the territory before heading downhill. If there are obstacles, avoid that part of the slope. Check carefully for snow-covered objects such as rocks, stumps, and branches.
- Never sled at twilight or at night unless the slopes are well lit and intended for night use.
- Warn your child not to push, shove, deliberately collide, or otherwise roughhouse while riding this equipment.
- Figure out beforehand how to stop the vehicle or get off safely in an emergency. For example, teach your child how to roll sideways off the sled if a collision appears unavoidable.
- Never use streets for sledding unless they are closed to traffic.
- Never slide through traffic intersections, across streets, or out of alleys and into streets—even if cars are not in sight at the time.
- Ropes should be held or tied on top of the equipment to keep them from slipping underneath and causing an abrupt stop.
- Never "hitch" a ride behind cars or snowmobiles while on snow equipment.
- Never slide downhill until the slope is clear of nearby sliders who could block the path. Move off busy slopes quickly after reaching the bottom.

14

Traveling Safety

One of your baby's first experiences is traveling—that
very first car trip home from the hospital

ONE OF YOUR baby's first
experiences is traveling—that very first car trip home from
the hospital. And because our society is very mobile, traveling
is a way of life at all ages, be it in a stroller, carriage, sling

carrier, or backpack . . . with a parent on foot, in a car, or on an airplane.

While we will discuss all these forms of travel in this chapter, there are a few basic rules that apply to all modes of transportation:

- Never leave your child alone anywhere, whether in a car, a stroller, a shopping cart—*anywhere.*
- If your child has grown past the stroller or carrying age, make a rule for hand-holding or sleeve-holding. Holding hands is most important when crossing streets or walking through parking areas.
- At the earliest possible age, teach your child to say his name, address (including city and state), and telephone number (including area code). When visiting very crowded places—malls, amusement parks, zoos, etc.— make sure your small child has full identification sewn into his clothing or in his shoe. But never sew this information on the outside of his clothing where a stranger can see your child's name and lure him into thinking he is a friend.
- Carefully read and follow the travel safety tips in this chapter.

Strollers and Carriages

One of the early experiences with your baby will certainly involve a little travel on foot, with the stroller or carriage you have selected (see Chapter 6 for safety considerations when purchasing). We'll start with a few basic safety tips in this area, beginning with the moment you unfold your stroller or carriage:

- Keep your child away from the stroller or carriage when you are folding or unfolding it—the moving parts are pinching hazards.

A well-equipped stroller

- Make sure your stroller or carriage has safety straps, and use both the waist and crotch straps. The challenge of climbing out of a stroller is irresistible to most children.
- Be very careful about hanging shopping bags, coats, or other items on the back of your stroller. If these things are heavy enough, they could cause the stroller to tip backwards. Also take care when pushing uphill because this could pose a tipping problem, too.
- Don't allow other small children to push your child in a buggy or stroller. They may not be strong enough to control it or safety conscious enough to know what moves could be dangerous.
- Never park your child in the stroller where there are things within her reach she shouldn't have. You can count on the fact that if she can reach it, she'll try to grab it, eat it, push it, or throw it—a child's most favorite pastimes. This could be dangerous to your child and, at best, embarrassing to you.
- Always use the parking brakes when you park the stroller or carriage. Especially make sure to use the brakes when you are putting your child in or taking him out.
- Never push or pull your child up a flight of stairs in a stroller or buggy. Carry your child and pull or push the empty stroller or, even better, have someone help you.
- When you are crossing a street lined with parked cars and have no traffic light for assistance, you should step out first and pull the stroller or carriage behind you so

you can check the traffic carefully before pulling your
child into the traffic lane. Also be very careful in parking lots—it's best here, when possible, to carry your
child and push the empty stroller.

Backpacks and Sling Carriers

When your baby reaches the age of about 4 or 5 months,
you may want to travel with her using a backpack or sling
carrier. Just remember that sling-type carriers without complete head and neck support and backpacks of any kind
should never be used before your child is at least 4 or 5
months old. You must be very sure your child's neck strength
is sufficient to handle the movements and jolts associated
with riding in this fashion. If you're not certain, ask your
pediatrician. Here are a few tips associated with the use of
backpack and sling carriers:

- Select a carrier that fits your child properly and is safe.
  Refer to Chapter 6 for information about selecting the
  right carrier for your child.
- If the carrier has restraining straps, use them at all
  times.
- Some backpack carriers have a stand so that you can
  put your baby in the carrier before putting it on your
  back.
- Never leave your child unattended after you have put
  him into the carrier.
- Never lean over when you're "wearing" your baby—in
  any type of carrier. Always lower yourself by bending
  at the knees. This will prevent your baby from sliding
  out of the carrier. It's also safer for your back.
- Check your carrier each time before you use it to make
  sure there are no torn seams, loose straps, or other signs
  of wear.

- Never carry your child in a sling-type carrier when riding in a car. If an impact occurred, your child could be crushed between you and the steering wheel, the dash, the door, or the shoulder belt.

These are just a few simple rules, but keep them in mind so your backpack or sling carrier will be used safely. When safety becomes second nature to you, you'll enjoy your backpack or sling carrier for its convenience, feeling of security, and closeness with your baby.

Sling carrier

Backpack carrier

Automobile Safety

As mentioned earlier, automobile safety begins at a very early age—with that first trip home from the hospital. On that trip, and on every trip, it is most important to make sure that your child is safely secured in a car seat. Once you have carefully selected the right car seat for your baby and have installed it properly in accordance with the manufacturer's instructions, the safety rule is simple: Make sure you use it every time your child rides in the car. Never hold your child in your lap while riding in the car.

TYPES OF CHILD SAFETY SEATS

There are basically four types of child safety seats: infant seats, toddler seats, convertible seats, and booster seats.

Infant safety seats are designed to be used from birth to about 9–12 months, or to a weight of about 20 pounds. This seat is a protective shell that cradles your baby in a semi-reclining position and protects her with a built-in harness. The carrier is fastened by the car's safety belt and must be installed so that your child is riding backward.

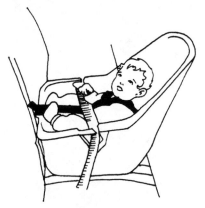

Infant safety seat

Toddler seats are for children who can sit up without support and weigh from 20 to 40 pounds. These seats are installed to face the front of the car. Most have a five-point harness which secures the child, and the straps are designed so that two go over the hips, two go over the shoulders, and one goes between the legs. Some toddler seats have shoulder and crotch straps attached to a padded shield, which takes the place of the hip straps.

Convertible seats are a combination of an infant safety seat and a toddler seat and can be used from birth to about 4 years old or a weight of about 40 pounds. The seat is installed facing backwards until the child is 9–12 months old or approximately 20 pounds, then the seat can be converted to a forward-facing seat. Convertible seats save money because only one seat is needed as your child grows, but these models can be heavier and more difficult to move than the infant-only and toddler-only seats.

Toddler five-point, shielded car seat

Convertible seat facing forward

Booster seats are intended for children weighing approximately 40 to 60 pounds. These seats are most practical for the child who has outgrown the toddler or convertible seat but is still too small to use the car's safety belt. Some auto booster seats are reversible and provide a medium height for

smaller children and a lower height for taller children—
which allows for proper placement of the shoulder harness
as your child grows. Here are three types of booster seats, a
harnessed booster seat, a regular booster seat that uses the
car's seat belts and a shielded booster seat.

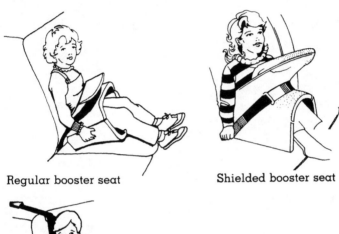

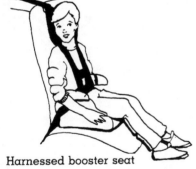

Regular booster seat

Shielded booster seat

Harnessed booster seat

SELECTING YOUR CHILD'S
CAR SAFETY SEAT

There are so many different car seats to choose from that
it can be a little difficult to decide which seat to buy. Here
are the most important rules to follow when choosing a car
seat for your child:

- When selecting a car safety seat, keep in mind that not all models fit all cars. If the seat has a safety shield, make sure there is enough headroom in the car to completely raise the shield. Check the fit of the seat in your car before you purchase it and remember that if it doesn't fit properly, you won't be able to install it safely.

- Select a safety seat that is comfortable for your child and convenient for you to use. The seat should be wide enough to allow room for growth and to allow your child to wear bulkier clothing. The seats that are easiest to use have only one fastener for the safety harness. Your child's safety depends on your willingness to use the seat every time your child rides in the car, so the easier it is to use and the more comfortable it is for your child, the better.

- It is unsafe to use a seat that is too large or too small for your child, so make sure that the seat is the proper style for your child's age, development, and size.

- Select only a certified safety seat. Travel beds and lightweight household infant seats have no safety value in the car and many car seats do not provide adequate protection. Check the label to make sure the seat meets Motor Vehicle Safety Standard No. 213. This means that the safety seat has been dynamically crash-tested according to government standards. If you intend to take your child with you on airplane trips, it's a good idea to select a seat that has also been approved by the Federal Aviation Administration (FAA). The airlines only allow safety seats with this approval to be used on planes.

- Some cars have seat belts with buckles that slide freely on the belts. This type of seat belt cannot secure a car seat safely because it loosens easily during ordinary stops and turning corners. For this type of seat belt you will need a locking clip to keep the buckle from sliding so you can properly tighten the belt on the car seat. If your automobile has this kind of seat belt, select a car seat with locking clips.

- Try to avoid buying a secondhand seat, but if you must, don't purchase a seat manufactured before 1981. Make sure the seat is really "like new." Look for cracks and dents. Check the harness straps for worn spots or missing fasteners. Don't use a seat that does not have installation and use instructions—write to the manufacturer for instructions and any recall information that may be applicable. If money is a problem, check with your doctor, hospital, or Division of Motor Vehicles. In many cities the local hospitals or service organizations loan, rent, or sell car safety seats wholesale.

INSTALLING AND USING YOUR CHILD'S SAFETY SEAT

Once you have selected the best and safest car seat for your child, a few rules apply for its installation and use. Follow them and you will find that not only is automobile travel safer for you and your child, but better behavior results.

- The back seat of your car is the place all the experts recommend you install a safety seat because it is the safest location. You may be tempted to put your child's seat in the front—especially the rear-facing infant seats—but don't do it unless close observation is needed and you have no choice. The best thing to do would be to sit in the back with him and have someone else drive or use a rearview seat mirror to keep an eye on him while you drive. The center of the back seat is the safest place for your child's seat, if the configuration of your seat belts makes this possible. But if your child's safety seat must be installed to the side, wedge a pillow between your child and the door and window as a cushion against any potential impact.

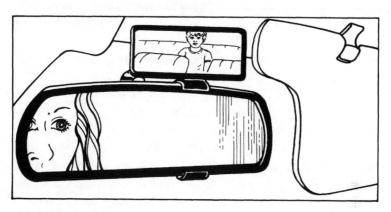

Rearview seat mirror

- If your child is still an infant (20 pounds or less), the infant safety seat or convertible seat must face the rear of the car. This will allow your baby's strong back to absorb the force of an impact or sudden stop rather than her more delicate chest and abdomen. When your child is very small, you may need to place blankets on each side of her head and at her crotch to support her and keep her from sliding down in the seat.
- Read all the instructions that come with your child's safety seat and follow them carefully, securing the safety seat with the car's seat belt *exactly* as directed by the manufacturer. If your child's safety seat requires a tether strap, it must *always* be used.
- Always use the harnesses or the front shield. If your child's seat has both, then both should be used. Adjust the harnesses to leave about an inch of slack so your child can move around a little, but don't let it be too loose.
- The National Highway Traffic Safety Commission recommends that you keep your child in a toddler or convertible seat as long as possible or at least until he

weighs approximately 40 pounds. Once he has out-grown the toddler seat, a booster seat is recommended until your child is about 60 pounds. Your child should stop using the booster seat when his ears are above the top of the car's seat back, at which point he'll be big and strong enough to use the car's regular safety belt.

Your small child is safer in a safety car seat than protected by adult seat belts. But if you find yourself in a situation where a safety seat is not available and your child is old enough to sit up without support, she is safer in the back seat using a seat belt than riding unprotected or in your lap. Tighten the belt snugly and as low as possible across your child's hips. If the shoulder belt crosses your child's face or neck, don't use it; instead, use the lap belt only. Never use things like pillows or cushions to boost your child in a belt.

There is an added bonus to using a car safety seat for your child. Researchers at the University of Kansas Medical School have proved that "buckled up equals better behavior." In several studies they observed children riding in cars with their parents. When not buckled up, the children squirmed around on the seats, stood up, complained, fought, and pulled at the steering wheel. When buckled into car safety seats, however, there were 95 percent fewer incidents of bad behavior.

They feel secure buckled up. In sudden stops and swerves, they are held snugly and comfortably in place. And, most car safety seats lift children high enough to see out the window. Children are less likely to feel carsick and more likely to fall asleep. With your child buckled up safely in his car seat, you will be able to relax and concentrate on your driving without having to divide your attention between the road and quieting your child.

Always remember that any child will learn by your good example. The best way to keep your child in the "safe-seat" habit is to buckle up yourself, every time you get in your car.

USE YOUR CAR SAFELY

While using a safety car seat for your child is by far the most important factor in automobile safety, many other general rules of use apply. Some tips apply to all car travel, while others may be especially important for longer journeys.

Car Safety Tips for All Trips

- Keep your car doors locked and when opening windows, lower them only halfway.
- Tape over the inside handles, locks, and window buttons so your baby cannot open the door or window.
- Never allow your child to play with the controls of the car—even if the car is parked.
- Don't allow your child to play with sharp or pointed objects when the car is moving. Pencils, pens, keys, candy or ice cream on a stick, and similar items can be dangerous in a moving car.
- Since your child will be riding in the back seat, it's a good idea to use a rearview seat mirror so you can keep an eye on your child without turning around while you're driving.
- To amuse your small child, select stuffed animals or soft safe toys. Tie them with short strings (shorter than 12 inches) to your baby's car seat. This will prevent her from tossing them out of reach or over the front seat to interfere with the driver.
- Make sure there are no heavy or sharp objects sitting on the back shelf or on the dashboard. A sudden stop or start could cause these things to fly off.
- Be very careful when closing the doors to make sure your child's fingers, feet, and hands are well away from the door.
- Never put your purse where your small child can reach it from his car seat. There could be many things in

your purse that shouldn't go into your baby's mouth—coins, lighters, cigarettes, combs, pencils, etc.

- On a sunny day, be sure that your child is comfortable and protected from the sun and glare coming through the windows. There are special auto sun shades that block the sun but still allow good visibility, and they can be moved from window to window as needed. Never hang a towel or blanket over a car window—this will create a dangerous "blind spot" for the driver.

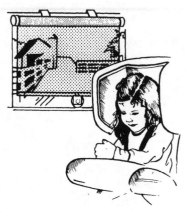

Auto sun shade

- Always try to park your car in a shady spot. Remember that metal parts and seats in a car can get dangerously hot in the sun, so check your child's car seat carefully before putting her into it. It's a good idea to use a blanket to cover her car seat in hot weather when your car is parked.

- Never leave your child alone in the car, even if you're parked in your own driveway or only plan to be out of the car for a minute or two. And never leave your car while your motor is running when there are children nearby.

- Make sure your child always enters and exits the car on the curb side—never from the street side. And see that you are there to escort him safely in and out, even as he gets a little older.

Car Safety Tips for Longer Trips

- Dress your child for the temperature inside the car. Remove her shoes and warm or bulky clothes so she will be more comfortable and have some room for movement.

- Never nurse your baby in a moving car while holding him in your arms. Stop the car, or sit next to your child while he is in his rear-facing car seat and make sure you have your seat belt on, too.
- Plan stops along the way so your child can get out and stretch—every one and a half to two hours is good.
- If your child is prone to car sickness, you can lessen this problem by keeping your car well ventilated and the temperature comfortable. If this doesn't help, ask your doctor about medication.
- Bring along plenty of things to amuse your child during the long trip. Depending on your child's age, these are good choices: a variety of soft toys, puppets, crayons and coloring books, storybooks or stories on tape cassettes, games without lots of pieces or hand-held electronic games. It's a good idea to provide things that are new to your child—this will make it more interesting to her and keep her attention much longer.
- It's wise to keep a small first-aid kit in the glove compartment or trunk, just in case of small cuts or insect bites.

Living Away From Home

If you are planning to visit someone whose home is not childproofed, or stay at a hotel, which is guaranteed not to be childproofed, here are some helpful safety tips to follow.

Put together a travel safety kit that you can use each time you plan to stay away from home. The kit should include:

- A safety nightlight.
- Portable electrical outlet caps and a roll of electrical or duct tape. While portable outlet caps are not recommended for daily use in your own home because chil-

dren easily learn how to pull them out, they are the most convenient for traveling because they do not require installation. See the section on electrical safety in Chapter 2 for information about the safest type of outlet cap. Take enough to cover at least 10 outlets for hotel stays and 20 for stays at someone's home or apartment. An alternative would be to use electrical or duct tape to cover the outlets. This tape should also be used for taping the connections of extension cords.

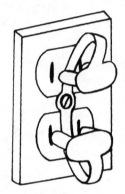 

Portable electrical outlet caps for traveling

- Five to 10 cord shorteners to wrap up electrical cords and keep them safely out of your baby's path. See the electrical safety section of Chapter 2 for more information about cord shorteners.
- Two or three safety doorknob covers or safety door latches. Remember that hotel bathrooms do not have high cabinets and you'll be putting your toiletries out where your child could reach them. So you'll want to make this room completely off-limits. Also, you will not want your child to have access through the exit door to the hallway. If you stay in a home or apartment, these door safety devices will be useful on doors to the bathroom, basement, garage, etc. Refer to the door safety section of Chapter 2 for more details about these devices.

- A high-chair safety strap or similar "safe-sitting" device. Many restaurants provide high chairs but not all of them have safety straps. And if the restaurant does not have a high chair and your child is able to sit up on her own, you can use the strap on an adult chair to secure your child.

- A poison first-aid kit, which should include syrup of ipecac and activated charcoal. Refer to Chapter 11 for more information about this subject. Also take along Appendix C's list of National Poison Centers (which has their phone numbers) and Appendix A's list of dangerous plants—or just pack this book!

When you arrive at your destination, install the safety devices you have brought along and go through each room checking carefully for potential hazards. Remove all breakable or hazardous items and put them away on a closet shelf. Move plants out of your baby's reach. Check the carpets and floors carefully for dangerous things like pins, coins, and buttons. Check to make sure your room and the building are equipped with fire and smoke alarms and that you know where the fire exits are.

The key factor in your child's safety when you are living away from home is to remain ever vigilant. There are so many new rooms with new things for your child to explore, and you can count on this to raise your child's curiosity to a new level.

APPENDIX A

Harmful House and Garden Plants and Trees

THE PLANTS, BUSHES, AND TREES LISTED HERE are considered poisonous and possibly dangerous. They contain a wide variety of poisons and, if ingested, the symptoms may vary from a mild tummyache, skin rash, or swelling of the mouth and throat to involvement of the heart, kidneys, or other organs. Do not assume that if a plant is not listed here it is not dangerous. Any Poison Control Center can give you more specific information on these or other plants that may be poisonous and may not be on this list. Keep in mind that many plants are not toxic unless ingested in very large amounts.

Poisonous House and Garden Plants and Trees

Cultivated Plants	Toxic Parts	Symptoms
1. **Caladium** *Fancy-leaf calad- ium*	All parts (Toxic substance: calcium oxalate crys- tals)	Intense irritation to mucous membranes producing swelling of tongue, lips, and pal- ate

Cultivated Plants	Toxic Parts	Symptoms
2. Colocasia *Elephant ear,* *Dasheen*	All parts (toxic substance: cal- cium oxalate crystals)	Intense irritation to mucous membranes producing swelling of tongue, lips, and pal- ate
3. Dieffenbachia *Dumb cane,* *Elephant ear*	All parts (toxic substance: cal- cium oxalate crystals)	Intense irritation to mucous membranes producing swelling of tongue, lips, and pal- ate
4. Monstera *Swiss-cheese* *plant, Ceriman*	All parts (toxic substance: cal- cium oxalate crystals)	Intense irritation to mucous membranes producing swelling of tongue, lips, and pal- ate.
5. Philodendron *Elephant ear*	All parts (toxic substance: cal- cium oxalate crystals)	Intense irritation to mucous membrances producing swelling of tongue, lips, and pal- ate
6. Caesalpina gillesii *Poinciana, Bird-* *of-paradise shrub*	Green seed pods (toxic substance: uni- dentified)	Nausea, vomiting, ab- dominal pain, and diarrhea
7. Convallaria majalis *Lily of the valley*	All parts (toxic substance: car- dioactive glycoside— convallamarogenin)	Local irritation of the mouth and stomach, followed by vomiting, abdominal pain, diar- rhea, persistent head- ache, and cardiac disturbances
8. Daphne mezereum *Daphne*	All parts, especially berries, bark, and leaves (toxic sub- stance: delphinine)	Severe local irritation to mouth and stom- ach, nausea, vomit- ing, diarrhea, and kidney damage

Cultivated Plants	Toxic Parts	Symptoms
9. **Delphinium** *Larkspur, Crow-* *foot*	All parts, especially the seeds (toxic substance: delphinine)	Burning and inflammation of mouth, lips, and tongue, followed by numbness; paresthesia, beginning in the extremeties, progressing to entire body
10. **Digitalis** *Foxglove*	Leaves, seeds, flowers (toxic substances: cardioactive glycosides—digitoxin, digoxin, gitoxin, and others)	Local irritation of mouth and stomach, vomiting, abdominal pain, diarrhea, cardiac disturbances
11. **Hedera helix** *English ivy*	All parts (toxic substance: hederagenin, or steroidal saponin)	Local irritation, excess salivation, nausea, vomiting, thirst, severe diarrhea, abdominal pain
12. **Hyacinthus orientalis** *Hyacinth*	Bulb; leaves and flowers if eaten in large quantities (toxic substance: unidentified)	Nausea, vomiting, abdominal pain, and diarrhea
13. **Hydrangea macrophylla** *Hydrangea*	Leaves and buds (toxic substance: cyanogenic glycoside—hydrangin)	Nausea, vomiting, abdominal pain, diarrhea, difficulty breathing, muscular weakness, dizziness, stupor, and convulsions
14. **Ilex spp.** *Holly, Christmas* *holly* **Ilex vomitoria** *Yaupon holly*	Bright red berries (toxic substance: unidentified)	Nausea, vomiting, abdominal pain, and diarrhea

Cultivated Plants	Toxic Parts	Symptoms
15. Ipomoea violacea *Morning glory*	Seeds (toxic substances: several alkaloids that are chemically related to lysergic acid diethylamide, or LSD)	Hallucination-like states, nausea, loss of appetite, abdominal pain, explosive diarrhea, frequent urination, and depressed reflexes
16. Iris *Iris*	Rootstalk or rhizome, leaves (toxic substance: unidentified)	Nausea, vomiting, abdominal pain, and diarrhea
17. Lantana *Lantana, Bunchberry*	All parts, especially the green berries (toxic substance: lantadene A)	Vomiting, diarrhea, weakness, ataxia, visual disturbances, and lethargy
18. Lathyrus odoratus *Sweet pea*	Pea or seed (toxic substance: beta-(gamma-L-glutamyl)-aminopropionitrile)	Slow and weakened pulse, depressed and weakened respiration, and convulsions
19. Ligustrum spp. *Common privet, Waxed-leaf ligustrum*	Leaves and berries (toxic substance: unidentified)	Nausea, vomiting, abdominal pain, and diarrhea
20. Malva sylvestris *Apple*	Seeds (toxic substance: cyanogenic glycoside—hydrangin)	Nausea, vomiting, abdominal pain, diarrhea, difficulty breathing, muscular weakness, dizziness, stupor, and convulsions
21. Narcissus *Narcissus, Daffodil, Jonquil*	Bulb (toxic substance: unidentified)	Nausea, vomiting, abdominal pain, and diarrhea
22. Nerium oleander *Oleander*	Leaves, stems, and flowers (toxic substances: cardioactive glycosides—oleandroside, oleandrin, and nerioside)	Local irritation to mouth and stomach, vomiting, abdominal pain, diarrhea, and cardiac disturbances

Cultivated Plants	Toxic Parts	Symptoms
23. **Prunus spp.** *Peach, Plum, Cherry, Apricot, Nectarine*	Leaves, stems, bark, and seed pits (toxic substances: cyanogenic glycosides)	Nausea, vomiting, abdominal pain, diarrhea, difficulty breathing, muscular weakness, dizziness, stupor, and convulsions
24. **Prunus virginiana** *Choke cherry*	Leaves, stems, bark, and seed pits (toxic substances: cyanogenic glycosides)	Nausea, vomiting, abdominal pain, diarrhea, difficulty breathing, muscular weakness, stupor, and convulsions
25. **Rheum rhabarbarum** *Rhubarb*	Leaf blade (toxic substance: oxalic acid)	Corrosive action on the gastrointestinal tract
26. **Rhododendron** *Rhododendron Azalea*	All parts (toxic substance: andromedotoxin)	Watering of eyes and mouth, nasal discharge, loss of appetite, nausea, vomiting, abdominal pain, paralysis of the limbs, and convulsions
27. **Ricinus communis** *Castor bean, Castor-oil plant, Palma christi*	Seed, if chewed (toxic substance: ricin)	Burning sensation in the mouth, nausea, vomiting, abdominal pain, thirst, blurred vision, dizziness, convulsions, and diarrhea
28. **Solanum pseudocapsicum** *Jerusalem cherry, Natal cherry*	All parts (toxic substances: leaves contain cardioactive substance solanocapsine; berries contain glycoalkaloid solanine and related glycoalkaloids)	Nausea, vomiting, abdominal pain, diarrhea, and hemolysis
29. **Taxus** *Japanese yew*	Seeds and leaves (toxic substance: alkaloid taxine)	Gastroenteritis and cardiac disturbances

Cultivated Plants	Toxic Parts	Symptoms
30. **Wisteria spp.** *Wisteria*	Whole pods or seeds (toxic substances: resin and glycoside wisterin)	Nausea, vomiting, abdominal pain, and diarrhea
31. **Arisaema triphyllum** *Jack-in-the-pulpit, Indian turnip*	Leaves (toxic substance: calcium oxalate crystals)	Corrosive action to gastrointestinal tract, producing swelling of tongue, lips, and palate
32. **Atropa belladonna** *Deadly nightshade, Belladonna*	All parts (toxic substances: tropane alkaloids, atropine, and hyoscyamina)	Fever, visual disturbances, burning of mouth, thirst, dry skin, headache, and confusion
33. **Cicuta maculata** *Water hemlock, Spotted cowbane, Poison parsnip*	Root and rootstalk (toxic substance: cicutoxin)	Increased salivation, abdominal pain, nausea, vomiting, tremors, muscle spasms, and convulsions
34. **Conium maculatum** *Poison hemlock, Fool's parsley, False parsley*	All parts (toxic substances: lambda-coniceine, coniine, n-methyl coniine)	Gastrointestinal distress, muscular weakness, convulsions, and respiratory distress
35. **Datura meteloids** *Moonflower, Angel's trumpet, Locoweed*	Leaves, flowers, nectar, seeds (toxic substances: belladonna alkaloids)	Dilated pupils, dry mouth, increased body temperature, intense thirst, confusion, delirium, hallucinations, and pulse disturbances
36. **Datura stramonium** *Jimsonweed, Jamestown weed, Thron apple, Angel's trumpet*	Leaves, flowers, nectar, seeds (toxic substances: belladonna alkaloids)	Dilated pupils, dry mouth, increased body temperature, intense thirst, confusion, delirium, hallucinations, and pulse disturbances

Cultivated Plants	Toxic Parts	Symptoms
37. **Gelsemium sempervirens** *Yellow jessamine, Carolina jessamine*	All parts (toxic substances: alkaloids—gelsemine, gelsemicine)	Cardiac depression, visual disturbances, dizziness, headache, and dryness of mouth
38. **Parthenocissus quinquefolia** *Virginia creeper, American ivy*	Berries and leaves (toxic substance: oxalic acid)	Corrosive action to gastrointestinal tract, nausea, vomiting, abdominal pain, diarrhea, and headache
39. **Phytolacca americana** *Pokeweed, Pokeroot, Poke salad, Inkberry*	All parts, especially the root, leaves, and green berries (toxic substances: saponin, resin)	Oral burning sensation, sore throat, nausea, vomiting, and blurred vision
40. **Podophyllum peltatum** *Mayapple, Mandrake, Ground lemon*	Rootstalk, leaves, stems, and green fruit (toxic substances: podophylloresin plus other compounds)	Abdominal pain, vomiting, and pulse irregularities
41. **Robinia pseudoacacia** *Black locust, White locust*	Young leaves, inner bark, seeds (toxic substances: a phytotoxin and a glycoside)	Nausea, vomiting, and abdominal pain
42. **Solanum dulcamara** *European bittersweet, Climbing nightshade, Deadly nightshade*	Leaves and berries (toxic substance: solanaceous alkaloids)	Vomiting, diarrhea, abdominal pain, drowsiness, tremors, weakness, and difficulty in breathing

Safe House and Garden Plants and Trees

The plants and trees listed here are considered essentially nontoxic or nonpoisonous. Plants that are commonly known by more than one name have been listed under each name. Harmful side effects from eating or handling these plants are unlikely; however, any plant may cause an unexpected reaction in sensitive persons.

Abelia
Abyssinian sword lily
African daisy
African palm
African violet
Air plant
Aluminum plant
Aralia
Araucaria
Asparagus fern
Aspidistra
Aster
Baby's tears or baby's breath
Bachelor buttons
Bamboo palm
Begonia
Birds' nest fern
Blood leaf plant
Boston ferns
Bougainvillea
Bromeliads
Burro's tail
California holly
California poppy
Camellia
Cast iron plant
Christmas cactus
Coleus
Corn plant
Crab apples
Creeping charlie
Creeping jennie
Croton—house variety

Dahlia
Daisies
Dandelion
Day lily
Dogwood
Donkey tail
Dracaena or dragon tree
Easter lily
Echeveria
Eugenia
Gardenia
Geranium
Grape ivy
Hedge apples
Hens and chicks
Honeysuckle
Hoya
Jade plant
Kalanchoe
Lily (day, easter, and tiger)
Lipstick plant
Lysima
Magnolia
Maidenhair fern
Marigold
Moneywort
Monkey plant
Monkey puzzle
Norfolk island pine
Pansy
Parlor and paradise palm
Peperomia
Petunia

Piggyback plant
Prayer plant
Purple passion
Pyracantha
Rose
Sansevieria
Schefflera
Sensitive plant
Sentry palm
Silver dollar plant

Spider plant
Swedish ivy
Umbrella
Violets
Wandering Jew
Wax plant
Weeping fig
Weeping willow
Wild onion
Zebra plant

Note: If you have a plant or tree that does not appear on either of these lists, you should move it to an area of your home that is off-limits to your child and contact your Poison Control Center for information.

APPENDIX B

Harmful Household Products

HERE IS A LIST OF COMMON HOUSEHOLD PROD-
ucts that should be kept out of your child's reach

Acid (anything containing an acid)
Adhesives
Aerosol cans
Aftershave
Air fresheners
Alcoholic beverages
Alcohol
Ammonia
Antifreeze
Antiseptic salves and ointments
Artificial-nail remover
Arts-and-crafts supplies
Automatic dishwasher detergent
Automotive products, including waxes and engine fluids
Bathtub and tile cleaners
Batteries
Birth-control pills
Bleach
Boric acid
Bubble bath, bath oils, and bath salts
Charcoal fire starter

Cigarettes, cigars, and butts
Cleaning solutions
Cleanser
Cologne and perfume
Cooking wine
Cosmetics
Denture cleaner
Deodorant
Deodorizers and air fresheners
Detergent
Disinfectant
Drain cleaner
Dry-cleaning fluid
Dye
Epsom salts
Fabric softener
Face creams
Felt-tip markers
Fertilizers
Fire salts
Flaking or peeling paint
Flavoring extracts
Flea powder
Furniture polish
Gasoline

Grease remover
Hair spray
Hair tonics
Ink
Insulation
Kerosene
Lawn recently treated with chemicals
Laxatives
Lead pencils
Lighter fluid
Lime and quicklime
Liniment
Lye
Matches
Meat tenderizer
Medicine
Metal cleaners
Mothballs, flakes, and sprays; camphor
Mouthwash
Nail-polish remover
Ointments and wipes
Oven cleaner
Over-the-counter medicines, including aspirin
Paint stripper
Paint thinner
Paints, stains, and varnishes
Pens
Permanent-wave preparations
Peroxides
Pesticides and herbicides
Pet foods
Pet medicines and vitamins
Petroleum products
Pipe tobacco
Plant seeds and bulbs
Plant food and fertilizers

Plants and trees—some (see Appendix A)
Powders, including baby powder and face or body powder
Prescription medicines
Prewash treatments
Razors and razor blades
Rodent and insect poisons
Rug cleaner
Rust remover
Scouring powder
Seasoning salts
Shampoo and hair rinse
Shaving cream
Shoe polish
Skin lotions
Soap and soap powder
Stain remover
Sulfuric acid (in car batteries)
Suntan lotion and oil
Swimming-pool chemicals
Tobacco
Toilet bluer
Toilet-bowl cleaner
Toothpicks
Turpentine
Typewriter correction fluid
Vinegar
Vitamins and minerals, especially iron
Wart remover
Washing soda
Water-softener salt or pellets
Wax and wax removers
Weed killer
Window cleaner
Wood preservatives

APPENDIX C

AMERICAN ASSOCIATION OF POISON CONTROL CENTERS

Certified Regional Poison Centers, November 6, 1990

ALABAMA

Children's Hospital of Alabama—Regional Poison Control Center
1600 Seventh Avenue, South
Birmingham, AL 35233-1711
Emergency numbers: (205-939-9201; (205) 933-4050; (800) 292-6678

ARIZONA

Arizona Poison & Drug Information Center
Arizona Health Sciences Center, Room 3204K
University of Arizona
Tucson, AZ 85724
Emergency numbers: (602) 626-6016; (800) 362-0101 (AZ only)
Samaritan Regional Poison Center
Good Samaritan Medical Center
1130 East McDowell Road, Suite A-5
Phoenix, AZ 85006
Emergency number: (602) 253-3334

CALIFORNIA

Fresno Regional Poison Control Center
of Fresno Community Hospital and Medical Center
P.O. Box 1232
2823 Fresno Street
Fresno, CA 93715
Emergency numbers: (209) 484-1222; (800) 346-5922 (CA only)
Los Angeles County Medical Association Regional Poison Control Center
1925 Wilshire Boulevard
Los Angeles, CA 90057
Emergency numbers: (213) 484-5151; (800) 77 POISN

San Diego Regional Poison Center
UCSD Medical Center, 225 Dickinson Street
San Diego, CA 92103
Emergency numbers: (619) 543-6000; (800) 876-4766
San Francisco Bay Area Regional Poison Control Center
San Francisco General Hospital, Room 1E86
1001 Potrero Avenue
San Francisco, CA 94110
Emergency numbers: (415) 476-6600; (800) 523-2222 (415, 707 only)
UCDMC Regional Poison Control Center
2315 Stockton Boulevard
Sacramento, CA 95817
Emergency number: (916) 453-3414; (800) 342-9293 (CA only)

COLORADO

Rocky Mountain Poison and Drug Center
645 Bannock Street
Denver, CO 80204-4507
Emergency numbers: (303) 629-1123; (800) 332-3073 (CO only)

D.C.

National Capital Poison Center
Georgetown University Hospital
3800 Reservoir Rd., NW
Washington, DC 20007
Emergency numbers: (202) 625-3333; (202) 784-4660 (TTY)

FLORIDA

Florida Poison Information Center
at the Tampa General Hospital
P.O. Box 1289
Tampa, FL 33601
Emergency Numbers: (813) 253-4444; (800) 282-3171 (FL only)

GEORGIA

Georgia Poison Control Center
Grady Memorial Hospital
Box 26066
80 Butler Street, SE
Atlanta, GA 30335-3801
Emergency numbers: (404) 589-4400; (800) 282-5846 (GA only); (404) 525-3323 (TTY)

INDIANA

Indiana Poison Center
Methodist Hospital of Indiana, Inc.
P.O. Box 1367
1701 North Senate Blvd.
Indianapolis, IN 46206
Emergency Numbers: (800) 382-9097; (317) 929-2323

KENTUCKY

Kentucky Regional Poison Center of Kosair
Children's Hospital
P.O. Box 35070
Louisville, KY 40232-5070
Emergency Numbers: (502) 589-8222; (800) 722-5725 (KY only)

MARYLAND

Maryland Poison Center
20 North Pine Street
Baltimore, MD 21201
Emergency Numbers: (301) 528-7701; (800) 492-2414 (MD only)
National Capital Poison Center (D.C. suburbs only)
Georgetown University Hospital
3800 Reservoir Rd., NW
Washington, DC 20007
Emergency Numbers: (202) 625-3333; (202) 784-4660 (TTY)

MASSACHUSETTS

Massachusetts Poison Control System
300 Longwood Avenue
Boston, MA 02115
Emergency Numbers: (617) 232-2120; (800) 682-9211 (MA only)

MICHIGAN

Blodgett Regional Poison Center
1840 Wealthy SE
Grand Rapids, MI 49506
Emergency Numbers: (800) 632-2727 (MI only); (800) 356-3232 (TTY)
Poison Control Center, Children's Hospital of Michigan
3901 Beaubien Boulevard
Detroit, MI 48201
Emergency Numbers: (313) 745-5711; (800) 462-6642 (MI only)

MINNESOTA

Hennepin Regional Poison Center
Hennepin County Medical Center
701 Park Avenue

Minneapolis, MN 55415
Emergency Numbers: (612) 347-3141; (612) 337-7474 (TTY)
Minnesota Regional Poison Center
St. Paul-Ramsey Medical Center
640 Jackson Street
St. Paul, MN 55101
Emergency Numbers: (612) 221-2113; (800) 222-1222 (MN only)

MISSOURI

Cardinal Glennon Children's Hospital Regional Poison Center
1465 South Grand Boulevard
St. Louis, MO 63104
Emergency Numbers: (314) 772-5200; (800) 392-9111 (MO only);
(800) 366-8888; (314) 577-5336 (TTY)

MONTANA

Rocky Mountain Poison and Drug Center
645 Bannock Street
Denver, CO 80204-4507
Emergency Number: (800) 525-5042 (MT only)

NEBRASKA

Mid-Plains Poison Control Center
8301 Dodge Street
Omaha, NE 68114
Emergency Numbers: (402) 390-5400; (800) 642-9999 (NE only);
(800) 228-9515 (Surrounding states)

NEW JERSEY

New Jersey Poison Information and Education System
201 Lyons Avenue
Newark, NJ 07112
Emergency Numbers: (201) 923-0764; (800) 962-1253 (NJ only)

NEW MEXICO

New Mexico Poison and Drug Information Center
University of New Mexico
Albuquerque, NM 87131
Emergency Numbers: (505) 843-2551; (800) 432-6866 (NM only)

NEW YORK

Long Island Regional Poison Control Center
Nassau County Medical Center
2201 Hempstead Turnpike
East Meadow, NY 11554
Emergency Number: (516) 542-2323

New York City Poison Control Center
455 First Avenue, Room 123
New York, NY 10016
Emergency Numbers: (212) 340-4494; (212) POISONS

OHIO

Central Ohio Poison Center
Columbus Children's Hospital
700 Children's Drive
Columbus, OH 43205
Emergency Numbers: (614) 228-1323; (800) 682-7625 (OH only);
(614) 228-2272 (TTY)
**Regional Poison Control System, Cincinnati Drug
and Poison Information Center**
231 Bethesda Avenue, M.L. #144
Cincinnati, OH 45267-0144
Emergency Numbers: (513) 558-5111; (800) 872-5111

OREGON

Oregon Poison Center
Oregon Health Sciences University
3181 SW Sam Jackson Park Road
Portland, OR 97201
Emergency Numbers: (503) 279-8968 (local); (800) 452-7165 (OR
only)

PENNSYLVANIA

Delaware Valley Regional Poison Control Center
One Children's Center
34th & Civic Center Boulevard
Philadelphia, PA 19104
Emergency Number: (215) 386-2100
Pittsburgh Poison Center
3705 Fifth Avenue at DeSoto Street
Pittsburgh, PA 15213
Emergency Number: (412) 681-6669

RHODE ISLAND

Rhode Island Poison Center—Rhode Island Hospital
593 Eddy Street
Providence, RI 02902
Emergency Numbers: (401) 277-5727

TEXAS

North Texas Poison Center
P.O. Box 35926

Dallas, TX 75235
Emergency Numbers: (214) 590-5000; (800) 441-0040 (TX only)
Texas State Poison Center
The University of Texas Medical Branch
Galveston, TX 77550-2780
Emergency Numbers: (409) 765-1420; (713) 654-1701 (Houston);
(512) 478-4490 (Austin); (800) 392-8548 (TX only)

UTAH

Intermountain Regional Poison Control Center
50 North Medical Drive, Building 428
Salt Lake City, UT 84132
Emergency Numbers (801) 581-2151; (800) 456-7707 (UT only)

VIRGINIA

National Capital Poison Center (Northern VA only)
Georgetown University Hospital
3800 Reservoir Rd., NW
Washington, DC 20007
Emergency Numbers: (202) 625-3333; (202) 784-4660 (TTY)

WEST VIRIGINA

West Virginia Poison Center
West Virginia University Health Sciences Center/Charleston Division
3110 MacCorkle Avenue, SE
Charleston, WV 25304
Emergency Numbers: (304) 348-4211; (800) 642-3625 (WV only)

WYOMING

Rocky Mountain Poison and Drug Center
645 Bannock Street
Denver, CO 80204-4507
Emergency Number: (800) 442-2702 (WY only)

APPENDIX D

The Perfectly Safe Library

THERE ARE BOOKS ON SEVERAL DIFFERENT SUB-
jects that every home with children should have on hand for reference. Listed here are favorites on each subject—the most complete, easiest to use, and most up-to-date.

*The Childwise Catalogue: A Consumer Guide to Buying the Safest
and Best Products for Your Children*
By Jack Gillis and Mary Ellen R. Fise
Published by HarperCollins, New York
This book covers all the conceivable products and services for
children, from baby shampoos and adoption services to health foods
and unsafe toys—thousands of items.

*A Sigh of Relief: The First-Aid Handbook for Childhood Emergen-
cies*
By Martin I. Green
Published by Bantam Books, New York
This best-selling book contains simple, easy-to-read instructions
for every common childhood injury from bites and stings to broken
bones.

*Baby-Safe Houseplant and Cut Flowers: A Guide to Keeping Chil-
dren and Plants Safely Under the Same Roof*
by John I. Alber
Published by Genus Books, Highland, Illinois
This book provides guidance to parents and others on eliminating
the risk of plant poisoning in households with children.

Dinosaurs, Beware!
By Marc Brown and Stephen Krensky
Published by The Atlantic Monthly Press, Boston
This book, which received a four-star review and the 1982 Notable Book Award from the American Library Association, uses an engaging group of dinosaurs to teach your child over 50 basic safety rules.

The Parent's Guide to Pediatric Drugs
By Ruth McGillis Bindler, R.N., M.S., Yvonne Tso, R.Ph., M.S., and Linda Berner Howry, R.M., M.S.
Published by Harper & Row, New York
This book includes all you need to know about the prescription and over-the-counter drugs you give your child from infancy through adolescence and how to administer them safely and effectively.

The Parents' Guide to Baby and Child Medical Care
Edited by Terril H. Hart, M.D.
Published by Meadowbrook; distributed by Simon & Schuster, New York
This complete, up-to-date guide offers treatments for over 150 common children's illnesses from "allergies to whooping cough."

The New Child Health Encyclopedia from The Boston Children's Hospital
Edited by Frederick H. Lovejoy, Jr., M.D., and David Estridge
Published by Dell Publishing, New York
Boston Children's Hospital, the largest pediatric medical center in the United States and the world's largest pediatric research center, designed this 700-page book for easy reference in any situation involving a child's health or safety: emotional as well as physical, emergencies as well as everyday questions, the most common ailments as well as serious diseases.

APPENDIX E

Resources for Child-Safety Information

American Academy of Pediatrics
Division of Publications
141 Northwest Point Blvd.
P.O. Box 927
Elk Grove Village, IL 60009
Ask for their set of brochures called "TIPP: The Injury Prevention Program"

American College of Emergency Physicians
P.O. Box 61911
Dallas, Texas 75261
Ask for information on poison prevention and emergency procedures

American Red Cross
Check your local phone book for the chapter nearest you; they have information on first aid, CPR, fire prevention, and water safety

Bicycle Federation of America
1818 R Street N.W.
Washington, D.C. 20009
202-332-6986

Commission of Public Health
Tel: 202-727-9870
Or write to: DHS Lead Poisoning Prevention Program
1411 K Street N.W. 12th Floor
Washington, D.C. 20005
Ask for their complete package of information on lead poisoning, including how to remove lead paint

Council on Family Health
420 Lexington Avenue
New York, NY 10017
Ask for their booklet "The Care and Safety of Young Children"

Food and Drug Administration
Consumer Communications HFE-88
Rockville, MD 20857
They have a comic book called "Dennis the Menace Takes a Poke at Poison" which is excellent for teaching children about poisons

Insurance Institute for Highway Safety
Watergate 600
Washington, D.C. 20037
Ask for their booklet "Children in Crashes"

Juvenile Products Manufacturers Association (JPMA)
Two Greentree Center
Suite 225
Marlton, NJ 08053
Ask for the free pamphlet "Be Sure It's Safe for Your Baby"

National Fire Protection Association
Batterymarch Park
Quincy, MA 02269
They have a catalog of literature on fire safety that is excellent for parents and teachers

National Highway Traffic Safety Administration
400 Seventh St., S.W.
Washington, D.C. 20590
Ask for information on child safety seats

National Poison Center Network
See Appendix C for the center nearest you; call your poison center for information on plants and trees

National Safety Council
444 North Michigan Avenue
Chicago, IL 60611
Ask for information on poison prevention and fire and bicycle safety

National Society to Prevent Blindness
79 Madison Avenue
New York, NY 10016
Ask for information about eye trouble in children and first aid for eye emergencies

Perfectly Safe
7245 Whipple Ave. N.W.
North Canton, OH 44720
(800) 837-KIDS
Ask for the free catalog of child-safety products

The Skin Cancer Foundation
Box 561
New York, NY 10156
Ask for their free booklet "For Every Child Under the Sun: A Guide to Sensible Sun Protection"

U.S. Consumer Product Safety Commission
Washington, D.C. 20207
(800) 638-2772
Contact them if you feel a product is unsafe or if your child has been injured by a product. Ask for their booklets "The Safe Nursery: A Booklet to Help Avoid Injuries from Nursery Furniture and Equipment," "A Toy and Sports Equipment Safety Guide," "CPSC Guide to Electrical Safety," "Children and Pool Safety Checklist," "The Super Sitter" (a good book to have your babysitter read), and "Which Toy for Which Child: A Consumer's Guide for Selecting Suitable Toys, Ages Birth through Five"

U.S. Department of Justice
Crime Prevention Coalition
Washington, D.C. 20531
Ask for their booklet "How to Protect Children"

APPENDIX F

Vital Statistics

THESE VITAL STATISTICS ARE NOT INCLUDED IN this book to frighten you, but to inform you. If you realize the potential dangers to your children, you will act to take the preventive safety measures to protect them.

- *The number-one killer of children today is not disease or drugs. It is accidents.*
  —C. Everett Koop, M.D., Sc.D., retired surgeon general

- *Every year, accidents kill and disable more children than kidnapping, drugs, and disease combined.*
  —National Safe Kid's Campaign

- *About 10,000 children a year die as a result of accidental injuries.*
  —Johns Hopkins University Injury Prevention Center

- *About 50,000 children a year are permanently disabled as a result of accidental injuries. This year [1989] one child out of four—19 million children—will be injured badly enough to need medical treatment.*
  —U.S. Public Health Service

- *As many as 9 out of 10 (90 percent) of all children's accidents can be prevented.*
  —All experts agree

- *Every year nearly 5,000 children under 4 years old die in the U.S. because of accidents. Most of these accidents could have been prevented.*

    —*American Academy of Pediatrics*

- *In a recent year, high chairs accounted for more than 9,000 accidents serious enough to require hospital emergency medical care. Most of the victims were under 4 years old and about 25 percent were children 1 year or younger. The majority of the injuries resulted from a fall from the chair when the straps were not used or the chair falling or collapsing on the child.*

    —*Consumer Product Safety Commission*

- *In the last four years [1985–1988] 25 accidental deaths in the U.S. were caused from automatic garage-door openers. Nearly all of them were children under 8.*

    —*Consumer Product Safety Commission*

- *An estimated 260 children under 5 years old drown each year in residential swimming pools and spas. Another 3,000 under 5 years old are treated each year in hospital emergency rooms following a submersion accident. Many of these submersion accidents result in permanent brain damage.*

    —*Consumer Product Safety Commission*

- *More than 25,000 children are treated annually in hospital emergency rooms for injuries associated with sleds, toboggans, and snow disks.*

    —*Consumer Product Safety Commission*

- *In a recent year, more than 16,000 children received emergency-room treatment for injuries associated with baby walkers. Almost all of the victims were children under 2 years of age.*

    —*Consumer Product Safety Commission*

- *More infants die every year in accidents involving cribs than with any other product intended for children. Thousands of infants are injured seriously enough to require treatment in hospital emergency rooms.*

    —*Consumer Product Safety Commission*

- *More than 1,000 infants and children die in car crashes every year in the U.S. and tens of thousands are seriously injured. Children under 6 years of age have the highest death and injury rate. Most of the deaths and injuries are blamed on improper use of safety seats—in only about 20 percent of the cases are the seat and the child properly restrained.*

  —Insurance Institute for Highway Safety

- *As many as 71 percent of the deaths and 67 percent of the injuries sustained in automobile accidents by children under 5 years old could be prevented with proper use of an approved child safety seat.*

  —National Highway Traffic Administration

- *An average of 90,000 children under age 15 each year receive hospital emergency-room treatment for injuries associated with toys.*

  —Consumer Product Safety Commission

- *Toothpicks cause over 8,000 injuries per year, most to children under age 14.*

  —Loraine Stern, M.D., Woman's Day, 5/30/89

- *Inhaling an uninflated balloon or pieces of a broken balloon is a leading cause of suffocation death of children.*

  —Consumer Product Safety Commission

- *In the U.S. every year, 400 children are killed and an additional 37,000 are injured in bicycle-car crashes. More than 300,000 other children are treated in hospital emergency rooms for bike-related injuries.*

  —Federal surveys

- *More than 1,000 people are killed in bike accidents each year—about half of them are young children. Studies show that as many as 75 percent of the deaths would not happen if the riders wore helmets.*

  —American Academy of Pediatrics

- *It's estimated that one in every 100 children under 5 years old accidentally ingest a poisonous substance each year.*

  —Poison Prevention Council

- *Every year, one in four children will be hurt badly enough to need a doctor's attention.*
- *It is estimated that about 600 button-type batteries are swallowed by children each year.*
- *About 8,000 children are injured each year in accidents involving lawn mowers.*
- *During the period 1984–1985 over 130,000 children between the ages of 5 and 14 were treated for baseball-related injuries.*
- *400,000 children each year are given emergency treatment for bike injuries. About 600 of them do not survive.*
- *Injuries involving playground equipment account for about 200,000 injuries each year serious enough to require emergency medical treatment.*
- *40 percent of all drowning victims are children under the age of 11. Children under 5 account for 3,000 near-drownings each year and more than 30 percent are left with brain injuries. 68 percent of the near-drownings take place during a momentary lapse in supervision.*
- *Diving and pool-slide accidents account for over 13,000 accidents per year to children between the ages of 5 and 15.*
- *Over 11,000 children a year are killed by cars. In 1987, car safety seats saved the lives of 200 children from newborns to age 4.*
- *For children ages 1 to 4, home falls are the leading cause of accidental death and serious injury.*
- *About 150 children die each year from fires started by playing with lighters (matches not included). Even very young children can get into trouble with a lighter.*
- *About six children die each year as a result of playing in a toilet.*
- *Each year children under the age of 4 are involved in over 8,000 bunk-bed injuries, over 24,000 sofa injuries, and about 48,000 chair injuries. The injuries are usually caused by a fall from the furniture to the floor or against sharp edges and corners.*
- *80 percent of all the poison-related emergencies can be treated over the phone by a Poison Control Center—if the parent is properly prepared.*
- *A recent Consumer Product Safety Commission study showed that approximately 65 percent of the containers with child-resistant caps were not effective.*

- *Poisoning is the most common medical emergency among young children. Most of the fatal poisonings occur to children between the ages of 1 and 3 years. About one out of every three childhood poisonings occurs at the home of a grandparent. On an annual basis it is estimated that one in every 100 children under the age of 5 ingests a poisonous substance.*
- *Most accidental poisonings occur in the morning between 10 A.M. and 11 A.M. or in the evening between 5 P.M. and 7 P.M.—when children are hungry, thirsty, cranky, or bored and parents are busy.*
- *About 41 percent of the poisonings to children are caused by prescription and over-the-counter medicines and vitamins; almost 40 percent of these children swallow drugs belonging to someone who does not live with them—usually a grandparent or babysitter.*
- *Every year in the United States, approximately 5,000 people are killed and over 40,000 are injured by residential fires. Most of the fire victims die from inhalation of smoke and toxic gas, not as a result of burns.*

Significant Facts

- *A young child can drown in less than two inches of water in a matter of seconds.*
- *A child can fall out of a window that is opened only five inches.*
- *A child can become entangled and strangle on a cord, ribbon, or string that is 12 or more inches long.*
- *In a crash at 30 miles per hour, an unbelted child would hit the dashboard with as much force as if he had fallen from a three-story building.*
- *Lawn mowers and trimmers have caused injury and eye loss to children playing as far away as 30 feet.*
- *Drinking mouthwash can cause a young child to fall into an alcohol coma.*
- *A young child can suffocate in a waterbed. If the bed is deep an infant can sink into it, turn over on her stomach, and be unable to turn herself back again.*

- *Nearly one in every six childhood scaldings occurs in the few hours that children visit their grandparents' homes during the holidays.*
- *Some children are needlessly burned because they believe clothes protect them from flames.*
- *More than 700 species of poisonous plants located in the United States and Canada are known to have caused illness or death in humans. Children are most often attracted to the colorful fruits, blossoms, and berries.*

Bibliography

American Academy of Pediatrics. *TIPP: The Injury Prevention Program.* Chicago: AAP, 1988.

American Academy of Pediatrics. *Family Shopping Guide to Infant and Child Safety Seats.* Chicago: AAP, 1989.

American College of Emergency Physicians and American Association of Poison Control Centers. *Emergency Action for POISONING.* Akron, OH: Children's Hospital Medical Center of Akron, 1989.

American Red Cross. *Independent Living Series: Home Safety.* Washington, D.C.: American Red Cross, 1984.

Arena, Jay M., M.D. *The Care and Safety of Young Children.* New York: Council on Family Health, 1988.

Arena, Jay M., M.D., and Miriam Bachar Settle. *Child Safety Is No Accident: A Guide to Safety Promotion and Accident Prevention.* New York: Berkley Books, 1987.

Bosque, Elena, R.N., M.S., and Sheila Watson, R.N. *Safe and Sound.* New York: St. Martin's Press, 1988.

Boston Children's Hospital. *The New Child Health Encyclopedia: The Complete Guide for Parents.* New York: Dell Publishing, 1987.

Child Safety Institute. *"Child Proofing": A Parent's Guide to Child Safety in the Home.* Port Washington, NY: Child Safety Institute, 1983.

Children's Hospital Medical Center of Akron. *And What About Plants?* Akron, OH: Children's Hospital Medical Center, 1988.

Cosco, Inc. *Travel with Baby: An Information Booklet about Choosing and Using Child Car Seats.* Columbus, IN: Cosco, Inc., 1988.

First Years, The. *Guide to Bathing Your Baby.* Avon, MA: The First Years, 1989.

Gillis, Jack, and Mary E. Fise. *The Childwise Catalogue.* New York: Pocket Books, 1986.

Guy, May, M.D., and Miriam Gilbert. *The Care and Development of Your Baby.* Chicago: Budlong Press, 1986.

Hayward, Mike. *Baby-Proofing Your Home.* New York: Lorevan Publishing, 1988.

Hull, Karla. *Safe Passages: A Guide for Teaching Children Personal Safety.* Dawn Sign Press, 1986.

Hurwitz, Sidney, M.D., Arthur Rhodes, M.D., and Henry Wiley II, M.D. *For Every Child Under the Sun: A Guide to Sensible Sun Protection.* New York: The Skin Cancer Foundation, 1989.

Insurance Institute for Highway Safety. *Children in Crashes.* Washington, D.C.: IIHS, 1986.

Juvenile Products Manufacturers Association. *Be Sure It's Safe for Your Baby.* Marlton, NJ: JPMA, 1987.

Metzger, Mary, and Cinthya P. Whittaker. *The Childproofing Checklist.* New York: Doubleday, 1988.

Miller, Roger W. *At-Home Antidotes for Poisoning Emergencies.* Rockville, MD: Department of Health and Human Services, 1986.

National Fire Protection Association. *Fire Prevention All Over Your Home.* Quincy, MA: NFPA, 1989.

National Fire Protection Association. *Let's Be Fire Smart.* Quincy, MA: NFPA, 1989

National Fire Protection Association. *Escaping Home Fires.* Quincy, MA: NFPA, 1989.

National Highway Traffic Safety Administration. *Child Safety in Your Automobile.* Washington, D.C.: 1989.

National Safe Kids Campaign, Children's Hospital National Medical Center. *Safe Kids Are No Accident.* Washington, D.C.: 1989.

National Safety Council. *Safety Bulletin No. 21: Solid and Liquid Poisons in the Home.* Chicago: NSC, 1984.

National Safety Council. *Safety Bulletin No. 92: Safe Use of Pesticides.* Chicago: NSC, 1984.

National Safety Council. *Ride 'em Safely.* Chicago: NSC, 1986.

National Safety Council. *Accident Facts.* Chicago: NSC, 1988 edition.

National Safety Council. *Family Safety and Health: Hot Tips to Protect You from Fire.* Chicago: Fall 1989.

National Safety Council, Home Safety Department. *Poison Prevention Program Kit.* Chicago: NSC, 1989.

National Safety Council. *Preventing Accidental Poisonings.* Chicago: NSC, 1989.

Ohio Department of Highway Safety, *Protect Your Kids in Safe Seats.* Columbus, OH: ODHS, 1985.

Perfectly Safe: The Catalog for Parents Who Care. N. Canton, OH.

Reader's Digest Association. *Success with House Plants.* New York/Montreal: Reader's Digest, 1983.

Shelov, Stephen P., M.D. "The Healthy Child: Beware of the Bugs," *Working Mother,* June 1989.

Stewart, Arlene. *Childproofing Your Home.* Reading, MA: Addison-Wesley, 1984.

U.S. Consumer Product Safety Commission. *A Toy and Sports Equipment Safety Guide.* Washington, D.C.: CPSC, July 1980.

U.S. Department of Justice, Crime Prevention Coalition. *How to Protect Children.* Washington, D.C.: USDJ, 1984.

U.S. Consumer Product Safety Commission. *Buyer's Guide: The Safe Nursery.* Washington, D.C.: CPSC, April 1985.

U.S. Consumer Product Safety Commision. *Safety Fact Sheet No. 43: Crib Safety—Keep Them on the Safe Side.* Washington, D.C.: CPSC, October 1985.

U.S. Consumer Product Safety Commission. *Which Toy for Which Child?* Washington, D.C.: CPSC, 1986.

U.S. Environmental Protection Agency. *Don't Bug Me.* Washington, D.C.: USEPA, 1987.

U.S. Consumer Product Safety Commission. *Safety Alert: Backyard Pool.* Washington, D.C.: CPSC, May 1987.

U.S. Consumer Product Safety Commission. *The Super Sitter.* Washington, D.C.: CPSC, 1987.

U.S. Department of Transportation. *Types of Safety Seats.* Washington, D.C.: National Highway Traffic Safety Administration, May 1987.

U.S. Consumer Product Safety Commmission. *Children and Pool Safety Checklist.* Washington,D.C.: CPSC, Spring 1988.

U.S. Consumer Product Safety Commission. *For Kids' Sake.* Washington, D.C.: CPSC, April, 1988.

Vandervort, Don. *Making Your Home Child-Safe.* Menlo Park, CA: Lane Publishing, 1988.

U.S. Consumer Product Safety Commission. *Product Safety Fact Sheet No. 74: Toy Boxes and Toy Chests.* Washington, D.C.: CPSC, 1988.

U.S. Consumer Product Safety Commission. *CPSC Guide to Electrical Safety.* Washington, D.C.: CPSC, 1989.

U.S. Consumer Product Safety Commission. *What You Should Know about Smoke Detectors.* Washington, D.C.: CPSC, 1989.

·perfectly·safe·

The CATALOG FOR PARENTS WHO CARE

To My Readers,

If you are unable to locate any of the child safety products recommended in this book, I invite you to send for your free copy of my *Perfectly Safe Catalog.*

You will find it a convenient one-stop source for products to help you with safety . . . for your child, your family, and your home.

The *Perfectly Safe Catalog* is the only catalog in America devoted exclusively to child safety. It is issued quarterly and is continuously updated as new safety products are discovered. You are assured that all the products included are of the highest quality and are tested not only by the manufacturers, but also by the Perfectly Safe Board of Advisors—real families, just like your own.

For your free catalog, just write to me today at the address below or telephone 1-800-837-KIDS. I will personally see to it that your copy is mailed to you at once.

Sincerely,

Jeanne

Jeanne E. Miller
President

P.S.: If you have any comments or suggestions, I would appreciate hearing from you. *Your* experiences are valuable to me in expanding my products and updating my book and child-safety tips.

Perfectly Safe
7245 Whipple Avenue NW
North Canton, OH 44720

Thank you. *J.*

Index